OHIO
THEN & NOW

CONTEMPORARY REPHOTOGRAPHY BY
RANDALL LEE SCHIEBER

TEXT BY
ROBIN SMITH

westcliffepublishers.com

CONTENTS

Acknowledgments

We are indebted to many people across the great state of Ohio and beyond for their help in researching and bringing this book to life.

First, thank you to John Fielder of Westcliffe Publishers for bringing us on board for this project. It's been a great experience, and we're happy to have the opportunity to show off our native state.

For help with photo and historical research, thanks to the Ohio Department of Natural Resources and its Division of Forestry; Julie Petersen, The Ohio State University Archives; Doris Porter and staff, Granville Historical Society; Pickaway County Historical and Genealogical Society; Margaret Piatt, Piatt Castles; Toledo/Lucas County Library; Paulette Weiser, Hancock Historical Museum; Nan Card, Rutherford B. Hayes Presidential Center; Sandusky Library and Follett House Museum; Defiance Public Library; Center for Archival Collections, Bowling Green State University; Linda Bailey, Cincinnati Historical Society Library; Virginia Weygandt, Clark County Historical Society; Clark County Public Library; Curt Dalton, Montgomery County Historical Society; Sunny Krugh, Mechanicsburg Public Library; Warren County Historical Society; Joyce Alig, Mercer County Historical Society; Bruce Greer, Stan Hywet Hall and Gardens; Linda Smucker, Pioneer and Historical Society of Muskingum County; Linda Showalter, Dawes Memorial Library, Marietta College; Pamela Speis, Mahoning Valley Historical Society; Mrs. Pat Stoltz, Geneva, Ohio; Darrin Lautenschleger, Muskingum Watershed Conservancy District; Gary and Susan Kaster; Mike Reddy and Bill Petrocci, American Electric Power; Amy Rutledge, Carroll County Convention and Visitors Bureau; Nancy Myerholtz, Waterville Historical Society; Judy Maniskas and Sam Sloan, Hocking County Historical Society; Dick Virts and Joe Rizzutti, Champaign County Historical Museum; Mary C. Krohmer, Lakeview Cemetery Association; Shirley Welsh, Enlarging Arts, Inc.; Mike Elliott, Akron–Summit County Public Library; William Mahon, Ohio Historical Society; Janet Oberliesen, Consulting Services, Worthington, Ohio; Ross County Historical Society; Friends of the Topiary Park; Art Smith, Parkersburg, West Virginia; Randolph Bergdorf, Peninsula Library and Historical Society; Ashtabula Marine Museum; John Miller, Archival Services, The University of Akron; and Larry Helton, The Society for the Preservation of Ohio One Room Schools, Middletown, Ohio.

Special thanks are due to those who went above and beyond the call of duty to help us with photo and general research: the Columbus Metropolitan Library's History, Biography, and Travel Department; Elli Bambakidis, Dayton Metro Library; Toni Jeske, Wright State University Special Collections and Archives; Duryea Kemp, Ohio Historical Society photo reproduction; Tim Manchester, J. H. Manchester Barn; Sr. Regina Albers, Maria Stein Heritage Museum; George Neargarder, St. Marys, Ohio; Julie Peterson, Mill Creek Metro Park; Fern Pickenpaugh, Pickenpaugh Studio, Caldwell, Ohio; David Tawney, Tawney Studio, Gallipolis, Ohio; Brooks Harris, Millersburg, Ohio; Maxine Spillman, Bolivar, Ohio; Sarah Vodrey and Phil Rickerd, Ohio Historical Society Museum of Ceramics, East Liverpool, Ohio; Janet Stephenson, Lakeside Heritage Society, Inc.; Daren Baker and Sara Johnson, Southern Ohio Museum; Frank Brusca, Department of Information Technology, Otterbein College; Sandy Day, Public Library of Steubenville and Jefferson County; Sandra Sleight-Brennan, Athens County Historical Society and Museum; and Marvin Case, Georgetown, Ohio.

Special thanks to the following for help with photo research and site location and access: Linda Paul, local historian, Findlay, Ohio; Bridget Garvin, Executive Director, Cascade Locks Park Association; Pat Metzger and Phil Nuxhall, Spring Grove Cemetery; Dick King, Old Fort Steuben founder, board member, and site manager; Wendy Waite, Stockport, Ohio; Floyd and Nancy Drake and the *Nancy Ann* sternwheeler; Joan Zerkle, Urbana, Ohio; Bryan Rayner, *U.S.S. Shenandoah* expert, Caldwell, Ohio; Whitney Bohan, Stan Hywet Hall and Gardens; Michael Hart, Mycle's Cycles, Georgetown, Ohio; Neil Sanders, Gallipolis, Ohio; Louis Andres, Malabar Farm State Park; Audrey and Orville Orr, Buxton Inn, Granville, Ohio; and Department of Development, Portsmouth, Ohio.

For generous site access, special thanks to: Nour Laasri and Diana Chambers, Renaissance Cleveland Hotel; Mike Yeager, Kentucky Transportation Cabinet, Roebling Suspension Bridge; Kelly Dentici and David Flocker, FirstMerit Bank, Akron, Ohio; Richard Stiff, National City Corporation, Toledo, Ohio; Ken and Jim McCall, Newell, West Virginia; Dan Sharp, Cabana Jacks, Sandusky, Ohio; Robert Morrow, The Crew's Nest, Put-in-Bay, Ohio; Rob McBurney, The Wilds; Scott Burin, International Towers, Youngstown, Ohio; Yvonne Eleyet, Washington Place Apartments, Columbus, Ohio; Bill Conlisk, Marathon Oil, Findlay, Ohio; and Joel Ashindorf, YMCA, Cincinnati, Ohio.

And finally, very special thanks to David Simmons, the editor of the Ohio Historical Society's *Timeline* magazine, who not only directed us toward some wonderful photo sources and great sites, but took the time to review the introduction to this book for historical accuracy. For all other historical material, we've made our best effort to check the accuracy of the regional introductions and photo captions. Any historical faux pas that may remain are all ours.

— RANDALL LEE SCHIEBER AND ROBIN SMITH

Harpersfield Bridge, Ashtabula County

Preface: Organizing Ohio

When Randall Schieber and I began to work on this book, neither of us realized just what a challenge it would be. As veterans of Ohio travel and tourism publications, we were both familiar with much of Ohio as it is today. As longtime residents and products of the Ohio school system, we were also familiar with the outlines of the state's history and its innumerable historical sites. As a photographer, Randall spends much of his time "on the ground" and possesses an amazing knowledge of Ohio places, famous and obscure, and of the roads and highways that crisscross the state. As a fascinated amateur historian and trivia nut, I had a good feel for where to find historical photos and lots of ideas about places that would make great then-and-now shots.

Well.

In "From the Photographer," Randall speaks to the challenges of finding usable, suitable historical images that could be rephotographed—not a trivial task, we discovered. Not that there is any lack of historical photos or sources to tap. No, the photographic challenges lay in the history and nature of our beloved Ohio itself. White settlement of Ohio began in the late 1700s. Before that time, the state was known only to Native peoples, who themselves had only had permanent settlements in the area since around the 1730s, and the odd white explorer or pioneer. Needless to say, neither group came equipped with cameras. Indeed, by the time photography became fairly common around the mid-nineteenth century, white settlers had been building cities and industries, rerouting rivers, clearing farmland, and cutting trees for well over 50 years. The photographic history of Ohio simply began too late to capture the original landscape or even early white settlement. Sadly, it was also too late to capture the native Wyandot, Ottawa, Delaware, Miami, Mingo, and Shawnee Indians who were gradually pushed out of the state by whites. By the early 1840s, Ohio's Native tribes, already restricted to tiny reservations in northwest Ohio, were forced to move west of the Mississippi River along with most other eastern Indians.

The alteration of Ohio's natural landscape by her early settlers also had an unexpected and often frustrating effect on our attempts to rephotograph many historic sites—but that's Randall's story to tell.

My first challenge was to sort through a mountain of possible photos and shape them into some kind of logical sequence. Randall and I spent many hours debating how to group the photos. We considered breaking them into cities, landscape, industry, and transportation, but that somehow seemed an artificial imposition on a complex natural and cultural geography. After much debate and thought about the themes that run through Ohio's history, in the end we decided to go with a regional division, which would enable us to explore each distinct section of the state as well as present the features that tie them together.

We have divided Ohio into five areas: southeast, northeast, southwest, northwest, and central. These are roughly natural divisions in regard to landscape and land use: For instance, northeast Ohio tends to be hilly and has been highly industrialized, while northwest Ohio is very flat and primarily agricultural. Though not as obvious or unchanging as the geography of each region, cultural divisions in the state seem to fall roughly into the same sections. One example is southeast Ohio, which is tied primarily to the old Scots-Irish culture of those who first settled its hills and ravines.

After choosing the structural divisions, we began our research with the Ohio Historical Society, which maintains a wonderful archive of historical photos at its headquarters in Columbus. Then we moved outward to more local sources of photos, of which there are many. Nearly all of Ohio's 88 counties have one or more historical societies and at least one large public library, many with their own photo archives. Local organizations also led to local collectors and even family photo collections. All of these sources yielded usable photos, graciously provided.

Overall and for each region, we found ourselves returning again and again to certain types of photos. City or town scenes, including streetscapes and prominent individual structures, were the most plentiful—perhaps not surprisingly, since parts of Ohio were already quite heavily developed when photography came along, and most photographers lived in the towns. Landscapes, including farmland, parks, and natural areas, were perhaps the most difficult. Farms in particular were a challenge. Agriculture was and still is extremely important here, but the older farms and buildings in the photographic record seldom remain in any recognizable form—although lovers of historic barns have managed to save some of these remarkable structures.

Other themes we pursued included historical sites, rivers and waterways, and industry. Transportation has also played a huge role in the history of Ohio and we included a large number of sites related to early highways, canals, railroads, and aviation.

We have provided a short introduction to each of the five regions, with its own brief history and points of interest. Then the photos: For each area, we have worked to show sites and subjects unique to that region as well as to include those that embody Ohio as a whole. For instance, the small cities and landscapes that became the hallmarks of southeast Ohio were also firmly connected to the rest of the state by the Ohio & Erie Canal, the National Road, and the Ohio River. In this region and throughout this book, we tried to capture both the individuality and interconnectedness of Ohio's places and people.

We hope we have provided a glimpse into the past and the present of Ohio. Each of the historical photos in this book is a window into a world that no longer exists, yet continues to define the present in the form of a building, a hill, a river, or a road. In a time when the alterations to our cities and landscapes seem constant, they give continuity to our lives. These pieces of the past are precious. Cherish them.

—ROBIN SMITH

From the Photographer

When Westcliffe approached me about doing this book, one of the first things we discussed was its overall look and feel. Ohio does not possess the wide-open vistas or majestic mountains of the western states in Westcliffe's "Then & Now" series. Not to worry, I explained. Ohio was a perfect candidate. Although it's more urban, with more industry mixed in with the landscapes, Ohio's rich history of growth and change would make for a fascinating book.

This more urban look also meant that I would have to use not just large-format photography, but also smaller formats such as 35mm and digital to capture some of the street scenes. One need only look at some of these photos in the book to see why. For many of the historic photographs, the photographer was able to set up his camera right in the middle of the street, needing only to dodge an occasional slow-moving Model T or horse and buggy. A century or more later, I was often at the mercy of much faster-moving four-lane traffic.

I also offered Westcliffe my assurance that finding the material would not be a problem. Ohio has many fine resources to draw from, including the Ohio Historical Society, county historical museums, and local collectors and organizations. However, as my collaborator Robin Smith and I were soon to find out, this process proved a little more difficult than we thought. Finding historic photographs that were suitable for this book meant being able to rephotograph them, as nearly as possible, from the same location and angle as the original photograph. The visual impact is startling when this occurs, both in the field as I am retaking the photo and when they align side by side in the book. But in Ohio, certain factors made it a much more challenging task than I first suspected (some 40,000 miles later, I can attest to this fact). Robin and I both have stacks upon stacks of photocopied historic photos that didn't pan out. The problem lies with our forests and trees and the fact that Ohio is currently more than 30 percent forested land.

Though more would be better, 30 percent is a big improvement over the turn of the last century. Farmers, builders, miners, and manufacturers cut down trees at such a rapid pace that by the 1890s the state—once thickly covered with hardwood forests—was practically timberless. At the beginning of the twentieth century, less than 10 percent of Ohio was forested!

This era also coincided with the development of photography, and many of the historic photographs taken at this time show a rather barren landscape. The photographer rarely had to worry about a tree obstructing his view in a street scene or a dense forest blocking the town below. Fast-forward to now, when trees are fortunately a common sight in our parks, alongside our homes, streets, and boulevards, and throughout much of the land surrounding our cities and towns. Thank goodness for their return, though they posed a very big problem for my rephotography of these historic landscapes.

Only 1 out of every 10 photographs that Robin and I found proved to be reproducible, many times because trees obstructed or completely obscured the scene. Many, many hills were climbed and many streets traversed to locate the sites of wonderful and telling historic photos—photos that, sadly, I simply could not rephotograph. However, reshooting the fine historic photos that you see in this book gave me such tremendous satisfaction that I soon forgot about the ones that didn't work. As you look through many of these images, you will clearly see the dramatic reforestation of the Ohio landscape—a complication to the rephotographer's task, but a welcome return for all Ohioans.

Two of Ohio's historic industries, coal and iron, also failed to yield usable photos, even though a good amount of photographic documentation exists of both. Disappointingly, after driving around to many of the old mining sites and blast furnaces with historic photos in hand, I found there was little chance of rephotographing what is left of them—again, due to the dense forests that cover much of the region today.

Oil and gas, another historic Ohio industry, was also somewhat frustrating to rephotograph. When I was growing up in Findlay, Ohio, I remember observing many of the beautiful old homes along South Main Street and having a vague sense of their ties to the state's oil and gas boom. As I worked on this book, I wanted to investigate the oil and gas industry much more thoroughly, realizing that it was important not only to Findlay's history but to a large portion of the state's. It also became an opportunity to visit my hometown and see how it has changed. While I was there, a local historian provided me with a priceless book on historic Findlay and engaged me in lively conversations about the town's past. The two South Main residential photos in this book are, in fact, from the Findlay book (see pp. 114–115). Unfortunately, very little is left, save a marker here or there, of the great oil and gas wells that once lit up Findlay's skies as well as the imaginations of people far and wide. But I think the grandeur of that era can still be imagined through the many historic homes that continue to grace the lawns of South Main Street.

I took an assortment of cameras and lenses on my trips. I also often carried with me a print scanner and occasionally some extended pruning shears. A collapsible ladder was always in the trunk of my car. We took only photocopies of the historic photographs out in the field to determine whether they could successfully be reproduced. A high-quality reproduction of the original photograph was then needed for the book if they panned out. Many of the smaller museums or private collectors had no means of providing this better-quality format, so my scanner came in handy. But even scanning posed its challenges. The beautiful Lakeside dock and beach house panorama in the Northwest section (see pp. 122–123) measured 4 feet in length. It took six separate scans, which I later stitched together on my computer, to get it into a reproducible form. This one as well as several others in the book were likely taken with a 10" wide roll Cirkut camera, the panoramic camera most widely used by professionals at the time. This large-format camera was able to produce a very sharp, 10" wide contact print. The drawback was that its method of capturing the image led to some perspective distortion. Other images, such as the 1866 panorama of Cincinnati on pp. 80–81, were taken in several steps and pieced together. All my panoramic rephotography was done in multiple steps.

The pruning shears I occasionally used for clearing certain overviews or cleaning up a little for a local park scene. Mind you, they were only employed very sparingly on obviously dead branches or wayward shoots and only in situations where a local park attendant would have eventually trimmed them anyway. For some of the overviews, my ladder provided just enough height over the trees to give me a clear enough view of the scene below. The Zanesville and East Liverpool panoramas (see pp. 18–19 and 64–65) would not have been possible without this extended height.

All of the photo gear and other equipment helped in accomplishing the physical task of rephotography. My knowledge of the state (I have photographed two books on Ohio and traveled it from one end to the other) was most helpful in choosing and locating many of the sites. Having the Internet's vast resources at my disposal was also a tremendous help. But the most valuable asset of all was Robin Smith, who kept things well organized and enabled us to meet our deadline. I am most grateful to her for her work on the text and captioning, for her help with locating many of the historic photographs, and for some great ideas on then-and-now photos. Her editorial and publishing background, vast knowledge of Ohio, and her sometimes humorous text added a dimension to the book beyond the photography alone.

Generally, the purpose of rephotography is to show objective change. My purpose was to subjectively draw the viewer into these changes. This consideration was important in the selection of many of these images. I wanted these juxtapositions to evoke a sense of wonder and surprise, or even amusement, and ultimately to inform and educate the viewer. This also meant that I sometimes chose photographs even though my rephotography could not always precisely match them. If now a tree, a branch, or a building blocked a part of the shot, changing my position slightly would help retain some of the key elements in the scene and tell the story better than if I had recorded the current scene from exactly the same position. Throughout the book, I have added my own occasional comments on the process of rephotographing a particular scene, which appear in italics after the caption.

Broad Street, Main Street, Market Street, Canal Street, Cherry Street, Walnut Street, Lincoln Street—I must have traveled down some 30 or 40 of each one of these popularly named streets and avenues in every city, small town, or village we researched for the book. Though they might share their names, each has a unique story to tell about its community's past and present evolution. It was from these streets—and the rivers, roads, hills, and hollows that led to them—that this book took shape. There were some trips that yielded no successful pairs, but even those that looked to be failures quite often led to my successes. Sometimes a trip to the local museum might yield no results at all, but their referral to a local collector down the street would yield some fantastic historical photos suitable for the book. Or their referral might not lead to any photographs but simply some engaging conversation about a fascinating part of Ohio's past. When stopping into Steubenville's visitor center, I listened for several hours to the story of Fort Steuben (Ohio's first military outpost). On another occasion, when I was looking to rephotograph a barn for one of the pairs for the book, I was graciously invited into the owner's home, which turned out to have been built by the founder of Urbana, William Ward, in the early 1800s; Ward once shared his home with the famous frontiersman Simon Kenton. For several hours, the current owners recounted legends about these two famous Ohioans. On neither occasion was I able to do any rephotography for the book, but on both I spent several enjoyable hours learning about Ohio's history. This was all part of the fascinating and enriching process of working on this book. I hope its photographs give the reader a deeper sense of what was then and what is now and convey some of the excitement and wonder that I experienced seeing it come together.

One final note: As the first settlers traveled up the rivers and moved through the dense forests of early Ohio, they initially devastated the land, cutting down trees for farmland and dirtying the air and rivers with pollutants from mines and manufacturing plants. You need only to go back to 1969, when the Cuyahoga River in Cleveland literally caught on fire, to see how careless Ohioans have been with their state. We have learned a lot since then, but still have a long way to go. But there is hope. Individuals can make a difference. Through the efforts of many concerned citizens, the Cuyahoga River and the land around it have been cleaned up. In 1974, the river valley, nestled between two of Ohio's largest metropolitan areas, Cleveland and Akron, was designated as the Cuyahoga Valley National Recreation Area. It was renamed the Cuyahoga Valley National Park in 2000 and remains one of the crown jewels of Ohio's parks. The Cuyahoga continues to wind its way through some of the most beautiful lands in all of Ohio, and I venture to say it won't catch on fire again.

As you look through this book, you will see many changes to our streets and cities and the lands surrounding them—some for the better, some for the worse. It is our duty to learn from the past and to wisely decide how to cherish our state and preserve it for the future.

—RANDALL LEE SCHIEBER

Consider a story from my college years. A friend came home to Dayton to visit family, bringing with him two school buddies, one from Long Island, New York, the other from San Antonio, Texas. Both were surprised when they arrived in Ohio. Bill, the Texan, had fully expected an urban maze. John, from Long Island, pictured cornfields from horizon to horizon. Chickens pecking in the streets probably wouldn't have surprised him.

Such are the varied impressions of Ohio, a state that sometimes seems to have no identity beyond, well, "Midwestern." So who was right about Ohio? Actually, they both were. Ohio is a place of contrasts. Had Bill visited Cleveland, he would have found exactly what he expected: heavy industry and a sprawling, multiethnic metropolitan area. Had John landed in rural northwest Ohio, he would have found those cornfields, interspersed with soybeans and tomatoes—though likely no roaming chickens. Of course, they might also have found steep Appalachian ridges dotted with abandoned mines and furnaces, as well as rolling, tree-covered hills; the Feast of the Assumption celebration in the streets of Cleveland's Little Italy and a German Oktoberfest; ore carriers unloading cargo at a Lake Erie dock and Amish farmers cutting hay behind draft horses; rap artists in a Columbus studio and an elderly fiddler playing tunes to which his Scots great-grandfather once danced.

Even before humans arrived in the Buckeye State, it was a study in geographic contrast. The sedimentary bedrock of the state was radically changed by a series of glaciers—most significantly by the Wisconsin glacier of about 25,000 years ago. At its most massive, the great Wisconsin glacier covered about two-thirds of modern Ohio along a southwest-to-northeast diagonal.

As the great glacier grew and then receded, it rearranged Ohio's topography like a box of blocks. Its final retreat left three distinctly different areas: the flat Lake Plains in the northwest and around the shores of Lake Erie; the Till Plains, consisting of the rolling hills and deep

Street fair elephants in the Miami & Erie Canal, Dayton, 1889

glacial debris, or till, that run in a diagonal strip across the center of the state; and the glaciated and unglaciated plateau areas in the east and south. The hilly, glaciated section of the plateau is the most populous area in modern Ohio, supporting both farming and industry with acres of rich soil and large deposits of gravel and sand. The unglaciated region in the southeastern corner of the state is a rugged and beautiful area of stony hills, ridges, ravines, and creeks, difficult to cultivate and thinly populated.

Ohio's white settlers added their own contrasts to the land. The first legal settlement in the Northwest Territory was established in 1788 on the Ohio River at Marietta by the Ohio Company of Associates, which was founded in Boston two years earlier. But the New Englanders at Marietta were probably already outnumbered by squatters who simply crossed the river from Kentucky and Virginia (now West Virginia), setting up housekeeping without benefit of legal title to the land. Southern farmers of Scots-Irish ancestry continued to make up the majority of settlers in south and southeast Ohio, forging cultural ties with the South and the rest of the Appalachian area that still remain today.

By contrast, northeast Ohio settlers hailed largely from New England, especially Connecticut. They brought with them their neat villages built around a common green. They also brought their family and cultural ties to the northeastern states, which have lasted to the present day.

Other ethnic and national groups were added along the way: Welsh miners in the southeast; German farmers in west and northwest Ohio; a group of refugees from the French Revolution in Gallipolis; Italians, Eastern Europeans, Irish, and southern blacks drawn to industrial jobs in northeast Ohio. Sadly, very few of Ohio's Native peoples have remained; they were nearly all expelled from the state by the mid-1800s. Still, today's Ohio is an ethnic gumbo to compare with New Orleans' best. Oompah music and wurst? Got it. Pierogies and polka? We have that, too.

Besides its topographic and cultural contrasts, Ohio is also a national crossroads. More than half of the population of the United States lives within 500 miles of Columbus. Ohio is connected to its neighboring states of Indiana, Michigan, Pennsylvania, West Virginia, and Kentucky by a web of interstate highways, including I-71, I-75, and I-77 running north and south, and I-74, I-70, I-76, and I-80—the Ohio Turnpike—from east to west.

That "connectedness" is not new. Transportation within Ohio and to surrounding areas has been an important aspect of Ohio's growth and history right from the beginning. In the early days of the Northwest Territory, Ohio's major highway was the Ohio River, which connected Pennsylvania and the East to the Ohio Country and points west and eventually found its way into the Mississippi River and down to New Orleans. Lake Erie provided the first access to northern Ohio, while the great rivers of the Ohio Country—the Maumee, the Sandusky, the Cuyahoga, and the Mahoning in the north and the Miami, the Scioto, and the Muskingum in the south—provided the first pathways into the interior.

As white settlement progressed, the need for land routes increased. By 1797, Zane's Trace was established as a route from Wheeling, in present-day West Virginia, across the southeast corner of modern Ohio to Maysville, Kentucky, by way of towns such as Cambridge, Zanesville, Lancaster, Chillicothe, and West Union. Though only a crudely marked forest trail that mostly followed old Indian paths, the route marked by Ebenezer Zane was nonetheless Ohio's first long-distance "road." By 1820, all the major cities of Ohio were linked by roads, most of them following old Indian trails and army routes.

Of course, that's not to say that travel along those roads was easy or even reasonably safe. Travel by stagecoach and horse in early Ohio was rough, dirty, and sometimes dangerous. Conditions began to improve a bit in 1825, when Ohio's best-known highway began construction. The National Road crossed the river at Wheeling and by 1838 had been completed across the state via Cambridge, Zanesville, Columbus, and Springfield to the Indiana border at Richmond, making road travel from east to west across the center of the state somewhat reliable for the first time.

Also in the early 1820s, planning began to link Lake Erie and the Ohio River with a system of canals similar to New York State's Erie Canal. Eventually, Ohio boasted two major canal systems—the Ohio & Erie in eastern and central Ohio, and the Miami & Erie in the west. The canals had much the same effect on Ohio that the railroads later had on the territories west of the Mississippi: They opened the interior to shipping, enabling farmers and manufacturers to ship and receive goods easily, and they stimulated the growth of hundreds of cities and towns, which sprang up to provide landings and supplies. Thanks largely to the canals, Ohio changed from an economic backwater to a mainstream economic center in the space of a few decades.

But the canal era was brief. The last sections of the Miami & Erie were opened in 1845. By the 1850s, the system had already started to deteriorate, and the state leased it to a private operator in 1861. After another decade of neglect, the state reclaimed the system in the 1870s. A long-delayed renovation of the canals' infrastructure was completed in the early twentieth century, only to have the great flood of March 1913 destroy much of the system. It was the death blow to Ohio's canal era.

Long before their final demise, the canals were losing ground to the railroads. The first rail line in Ohio linked Toledo to Adrian, Michigan, in 1836. By 1860, Ohio had more track mileage than any other state in the Union—2,974 miles. The speedy rail lines linked even

Train depot, Zanesville

small towns, not only to Ohio's larger cities but to the rest of the United States, and remained Ohio's principal mode of travel until the rise of the automobile in the twentieth century. From the 1890s to the 1930s, the railroads were joined by dozens of electric interurban rail lines offering fast, cheap passenger and freight service between even the smallest towns.

Today interstate highways and air travel (a mode pioneered by Ohioans Wilbur and Orville Wright) have erased the canal system and interurbans and greatly diminished the railroads. But scattered remnants of those earlier means of transportation remain. Sections of the canals have been restored as parks, abandoned locks and aqueducts haunt the landscape, and feeder lakes have become recreational areas. The interurbans and railroads left a legacy of bridges, tunnels, and beautiful old train stations. Though many large stations were destroyed in the urban renewal craze of the 1960s, a few were saved from the wrecking ball and restored to at least an echo of their former glory.

Traces of the old highways also remain. Sections of the National Road still exist as US 40, now closely paralleled by I-70 across the state. The original route of Zane's Trace is loosely followed by sections of I-70, US 22, US 50, OH 159, and OH 41.

But back to my college story. The punch line is that whatever you expect to find in Ohio, you probably will find—somewhere. Our state is a mixed bag geographically, ethnically, and culturally. We Buckeyes (no jokes about worthless nuts, please) are tied together by our lakes, our rivers, our highways, and the shared history of our beautiful state. I hope that with this book, Randall and I can convey to you, the reader, some of that beauty and rich history to be found within the borders of Ohio—then and now.

—ROBIN SMITH

Southeast Ohio

In April 1788, 48 men from the Ohio Company of Associates pulled ashore at the confluence of the Muskingum and Ohio Rivers and established the first legal white settlement in what would become Ohio. The Company had purchased 1,781,760 acres of the Northwest Territory from Congress for what worked out to be about 8.5 cents per acre. The orderly New Englanders were only the latest settlers to arrive, of course. Enterprising Kentuckians and Virginians had already begun moving up the river valleys.

Southeast Ohio is nearly all rugged, unglaciated plateau, and its deep river gorges and scarce farmland made settlement a challenge. What the region *did* offer was coal, iron ore, oil, and natural gas in large quantities. Commercial mining of coal began around 1800. As part of the famous Hanging Rock Iron Region, southeast Ohio also produced tons of iron from the early 1800s until the area's last blast furnace stopped production in 1916. The hills were nearly stripped clean of timber by the end of the Civil War, much of it used to produce charcoal to fire the furnaces.

In 1814, Noble County saw the first discovery of oil in a drilled well, and the state's first commercial oil well began production in 1860 in Washington County. Large patches of oil and gas remain in the region, especially in Morgan, Muskingum, Meigs, and Athens Counties.

In a landscape unsuited for large cities, southeast Ohio is a place of small towns and tiny hamlets. The three largest cities, Chillicothe, Zanesville, and Portsmouth, are found around the edges of the rougher regions, while smaller Marietta, Logan, and Athens nestle into the hills.

Southeast Ohio's early development was swift, but the decline of local iron forges in the late 1800s and then the steel and coal industries in the 1960s left the area economically depressed and sprinkled with deserted furnaces, mines, and towns. In the 1930s, the

Stockport Mill, Muskingum Dam, and Lock 6, Stockport, circa 1900

Wreck of the U.S.S. Shenandoah *dirigible near Ava, September 1925*

U.S. Forest Service began purchasing and reclaiming the Wayne National Forest. As trees have returned to the rugged, beautiful hills, tourism has become a major part of the regional economy.

For all its difficulties, this area of the Buckeye State demonstrates the resilience of the land and the people who call it home. Through flood and fire, downturn and resurgence, southeast Ohio remains the heart of the beauty that is Ohio.

Marietta from Harmar Hill, circa 1898 (Washington County)

Ohio's first legal settlement was established in 1788 on the east bank of the Muskingum River at its confluence with the Ohio River. One hundred and ten years later, the thriving city of Marietta was photographed from Harmar Hill looking east across the Muskingum. The commercial buildings along Front Street are visible beyond the Putnam Street Bridge. To the right of the bridge is Lock 1 on the Muskingum River; the Phoenix Mill is next to the railroad bridge. At the upper right, the Ohio River curves into the distance. The rounded tower visible above the tip of Buckley Island (just right of center) is the Bellevue Hotel.

    Today several of the Front Street buildings still stand, and the revamped Putnam Street Bridge is still the primary crossing between downtown and Harmar Hill. The Phoenix Mill is gone, as is the river lock, which was dismantled after the construction of dams on the Ohio River raised the water level in the Muskingum and made the lock unnecessary. The Ohio River bridge that is nearest the camera is the Williamstown Bridge, which carries auto traffic between Marietta and Williamstown, West Virginia.

Ohio River Levee, Marietta, 1911 (Washington County)

As in many river towns, Marietta's levee is an important gathering spot. In the heyday of river sternwheelers, the boats moored at the Ohio River levee to unload passengers and goods. The levee became an entertainment venue when showboats visited. The crowd in this photo was awaiting the arrival of the *New Orleans* on November 6, 1911. The building to the left with the tower is the Bellevue Hotel; its taller neighbor is the Riverview Building, which offered great river views from its office windows.

Marietta still plays host to riverboats during the annual Ohio River Sternwheeler Festival, when dozens of sternwheelers tie up at the levee. In September 2004, the festival took place during the high-water remnants of Hurricane Frances, which flooded many sections of Marietta. Only a few weeks later, rains from Hurricane Ivan swept up the Ohio Valley, raising the river to 44.97 feet. The former Bellevue Hotel, renamed the Lafayette Hotel in 1918, had nearly a foot of water in its lobby. Another veteran survivor of river floods, the Riverview Building still stands across from the Lafayette.

PHOTOGRAPHER *I had intended to rephotograph the 1911 photograph of the levee from one of the sternwheelers during the Sternwheeler Festival. Because of floodwater from Hurricane Frances, however, the few sternwheelers that had managed to come downriver had to tie up precariously to the shoreline where the levee normally stood. They rode out the high water and the festival was held in downtown Marietta instead of on the levee. I took these inset photos from the Williamstown Bridge during the high water and used a photograph I had taken a few years earlier for my "now" (main photo, above). Although a compromise for a true "then and now," I think they still make an interesting pair.*

Williamstown Bridge, Marietta, 1903 (Washington County)

When the original Williamstown Bridge was built in 1903, it presented a major construction challenge: erecting the bridge over the riverboat channel north of Buckley Island without obstructing river traffic. The problem was solved by building the south section of the bridge from West Virginia to the center pier first. That portion of the span then served as a counterweight, allowing the north section to be cantilevered over the river.

The Williamstown Bridge was originally erected to carry streetcar traffic across the river between Marietta and Williamstown, but eventually became an automobile bridge. The 1903 structure was closed in the 1980s and replaced by this modern steel span in the 1990s.

Confluence of the Ohio and Muskingum Rivers, Marietta, late 1800s (Washington County)

This confluence was a major reason the Ohio Company established its settlement at Marietta. The Ohio River was already the major waterway to the Northwest Territory, and the Muskingum provided access to the interior country. As larger vessels appeared on the Ohio and the population in the area increased, a series of dams and 11 locks were built on the Muskingum to facilitate shipping and tie the river into the Ohio & Erie Canal near Dresden. The dams also prevented seasonal low water on the Muskingum.

A series of dams and other channel improvements now ensure deep enough water in the Ohio for commercial traffic all year. They have also changed the bank of the river tremendously; gone are the low dirt banks where the wagon in the old photo waited for riverboats to land.

Lock 3, Lowell, circa 1907 (Washington County)

The Lowell Lock was one of 11 locks built on the Muskingum River between 1837 and 1841. The citizens of the Muskingum River valley were furious when the Ohio & Erie Canal project bypassed their river in favor of a longer route that would take the canal through Chillicothe, which had more political clout in the state legislature. In 1836, an enlarged canal system plan called for connecting the canal to the Muskingum River at Dresden, which provided two routes to the Ohio River from Cleveland—the Muskingum route through Marietta and the longer canal route through Chillicothe and Portsmouth.

Today the Muskingum River locks are believed to be the only remaining hand-operated lock system in the world. Lock 1 at Marietta was dismantled after Ohio River improvements made it unnecessary, but the remaining 10 locks are used by recreational boaters on the Muskingum. The entire system is now a part of the Muskingum River Parkway, a state park that stretches from Coshocton to Marietta.

PHOTOGRAPHER *This new view of the Lowell Lock showcases how much more of the landscape is forested now than at the turn of the century. I photographed the sternwheeler* Nancy Ann, *owned by Floyd and Nancy Drake, as it approached the locks.*

McConnelsville Opera House, McConnelsville, circa 1920s (Morgan County)

The McConnelsville Opera House was the first building in Morgan County to be completely lit by electricity. When it opened in 1892 with a performance of *The Mikado,* many in the audience were as anxious to see the electric lights as Gilbert and Sullivan's comic opera. "Opera house" is a bit of a misnomer, here as in hundreds of small towns across Ohio. The halls were more likely to host traveling theatricals, comedy, and musical acts than opera, but an opera house was a respectable place to go, while a "theater" would have been considered tawdry.

The opera house continues to host both film and live performances. The current seats and stage curtains date from the 1930s and were restored in the 1990s. The building still retains its original hardwood floors and the original footlights around the edge of the stage.

Muskingum County Courthouse, Zanesville, circa 1905 (Muskingum County)

Muskingum County's grand old courthouse opened in 1877, replacing "Old 1809," the former courthouse and state capitol (1810–1812) that stood on the same site. A large fountain on the front esplanade featured three half-nude maidens gazing into the water, inspiring immediate complaints about the immoral influence of topless females on the county's youth. The maidens prevailed for a number of years, but in 1903 the fountain was removed, sold for scrap metal, and replaced by the flower garden in this photo. A Miss Goodlive of Prospect Avenue reportedly bought two of the maidens and installed them in her home garden. The reaction of the county's young men is not recorded.

Along with the loss of much of its elaborate ironwork and statuary, the courthouse has survived a number of mishaps. The 1913 flood dumped 2 feet of water into the ground floor; in 1879 and 1914, falling clock weights from the tower punched into the second-floor ceilings. The 1940s brought an invasion of starlings to the third floor, and the building suffered a fire in 1955. Through it all, the courthouse tower has remained a beacon on the Zanesville skyline.

Zanesville (Muskingum County)
circa 1895

Zanesville was founded in 1797 by John McIntire at the confluence of the Licking and Muskingum Rivers. The land was deeded by his father-in-law, Ebenezer Zane, and lay along Zane's Trace, Ohio's first major road. The later National Road also passed through Zanesville along the same route, making the city a natural transportation hub for both road and river traffic. The first photo was probably taken shortly before the turn of the twentieth century, looking roughly north. The third incarnation of Zanesville's famous Y-bridge crosses the rivers at left, and the clock tower of the Muskingum County Courthouse appears in the right third of the photo.

The second photo was taken after the disastrous 1913 flood. Most of the structures on the riverbank have been swept away, including the railroad and highway bridges at the right edge of the photo. The fourth Y-bridge, a concrete structure, survived, as did the county courthouse.

Trees screen large parts of the current view, but the confluence of the rivers appears largely unchanged. The current Y-bridge still crosses the rivers at the left, and the rebuilt railroad bridge and courthouse appear in the right third of the image. Other survivors include the large Amazon Coffee and Spice Mills building near the center of the 1913 photo and the multistory dark brick building to the left of the courthouse.

Y-bridge, Zanesville (Muskingum County)

circa 1890

circa 1902–1910

The Y-bridge is Zanesville's claim to highway fame. The structure has fascinated visitors ever since it first opened in 1814 as a toll bridge and has spawned multiple jokes involving travelers who are given directions to "go to the middle of the bridge and turn left." The first wooden bridge collapsed into the river in 1818, leaving only its central pier. The second bridge was partially washed away by a flood in 1832 and replaced by the covered bridge in the first photo, which became a free bridge in 1866.

In 1900, inspectors informed the city fathers of Zanesville that the Y-bridge was "in a dangerous condition and a constant menace to public safety." In the fall of that year, demolition began on the wooden bridge, revealing dozens of old coins in the central pier that had fallen through the cracks in the wooden deck around the old toll house. The reinforced concrete bridge in the second photo opened in 1902. It was completely covered in the 1913 flood, but survived despite having its concrete railings pounded off by floating debris.

In 1984, Zanesville opened the fifth edition of the Y-bridge. The industrial buildings in the foreground no longer stand and the buggies and streetcars are long gone, but Zanesville's most famous landmark continues to carry US 40 traffic across the river confluence.

S-bridge, New Concord, circa 1925–1930 (Muskingum County)

S-bridges were an odd feature of the original National Road. This bridge over Fox Creek just west of New Concord was completed about 1828 and was upgraded to brick paving to provide a better surface for military vehicles in 1919. By the time this photo was taken, the old bridge had been bypassed by the new, wider US 40 at left.

Theories abound about the reasons for S-bridges, from bar bets by engineers to slowing traffic—although it's hard to imagine having to slow down a horse and buggy for a safe bridge crossing. The real reason for the S-bridges was to route the main portion of the bridge across a waterway at right angles, allowing a shorter, less expensive span. The old S-bridge at New Concord is now a roadside historical site. Visitors can see five different transportation routes from the bridge: Zane's Trace, the National Road, the B&O Railroad, US 40, and I-70. There is also an original National Road mile marker at the site.

National Road, Cambridge, 1932 (Guernsey County)

Cambridge is best known as the home of the Cambridge Glass Company, which turned out fine art glass from 1902 to 1954. But before glass, the area was also known for coal mining, pottery, chair making, and buggy manufacturing. One of the reasons for Cambridge's quick early growth was its position on Zane's Trace and, later, the National Road. This view looks west in 1932. The National Road turns left at the fork in the road, curves around, and continues westward toward Zanesville through the deep cut in the hills seen in the background.

Today Cambridge sits at the interchange of I-70 and I-77, shifting most traffic away from the National Road (now US 40). This intersection looks much as it did 60 years ago, with many of the old buildings still standing. The trees and other vegetation have covered the raw stone in the background, but the road cut is still visible as a dip in the trees.

Conkle's Hollow State Nature Preserve, 1939 (Hocking County)

The deep sandstone gorges, cliffs, and waterfalls of the Hocking Hills make up some of Ohio's most spectacular landscapes. The gorges were formed thousands of years ago by floodwaters from the melting Wisconsin glacier. Torrents of water poured through cracks in the hard top layer of rock and left deep tunnels through the soft lower layers. Eventually the roofs of the tunnels collapsed, forming gorges with high cliff walls and dozens of recess caves.

Conkle's Hollow is a spectacular Black Hand sandstone gorge carved out by Pine Creek. In some places, cliffs rise nearly 200 feet tall from the deep, cool gorge, which shelters wildflower and fern communities. The state of Ohio purchased Conkle's Hollow in 1925 to preserve the beauty of the area. In 1977, Conkle's Hollow was dedicated as a state nature preserve, enabling the Ohio Department of Natural Resources to better manage and protect the plant and animal populations in the area. This scene has changed little in nearly 70 years.

Trail to Lower Falls, Old Man's Cave, circa 1930–1950 (Hocking County)

Old Man's Cave is named for Richard Rowe, a reclusive trapper who lived there in the first half of the nineteenth century. Legend has it that Rowe accidentally shot himself while breaking ice in a stream with the butt of his musket and is buried somewhere in the gorge. The pioneer families in the area encouraged their children to stay away from the area's dangerous cliffs by telling them the "old man's ghost" lived there. The area quickly became Old Man's Gorge, then Old Man's Cave. In 1924, Old Man's Cave was part of the first 146-acre purchase in the area by the state of Ohio. When this photo was taken, the state had already improved the trails and access to the area.

Time seems to move slowly in the Hocking Hills. The only obvious changes in the new photo are the trail identification sign and the clothing style. Old Man's Cave is still the best known of the five areas that make up Hocking Hills State Park and draws thousands of visitors annually to such features as the Upper and Lower Falls areas and the Devil's Bathtub.

Rock House, circa 1930–1950 (Hocking County)

This steep trail leads to Rock House, a cavelike rock formation once used as a shelter by both Indians and white settlers. The Indians carved out two small hollows in the sandstone shelves, where they distilled medicinal turpentine from bits of pitch pine wood. When whites moved into the area in the late 1700s, they also used the stills. The only recorded death from a bear attack in Hocking County occurred at Rock House in 1863: William Reynolds, a herdsman who sheltered his animals in the Rock House, was attacked on the trail on his way to care for his stock and died a week later.

Today the Rock House trail is one of the more challenging hikes in Hocking Hills State Park, but the beauty of the area is the reward for those who take it. The two turpentine stills remain after 300 years, mute reminders of the lives that passed through Rock House and the Hocking Hills many years ago. The inset photo was taken looking out of Rock House. The opening is just beyond the right edge of the larger photos above.

Cedar Falls, 1908 (Hocking County)

Cedar Falls should really be "Hemlock Falls," but the early settlers who named the site mistook the area's beautiful hemlocks for cedar trees and the name stuck. Cedar Falls and its gorge were well-known to the local Indians, who found saltpeter for curing meat in one of the gorge's caves. In the early 1800s, there was a trading post just downstream from the falls that served both the Indians and their white neighbors. In 1835, a gristmill was built above the falls.

A part of Hocking Hills State Park, Cedar Falls is the most photographed waterfall in Hocking County and has appeared in dozens of books, magazines, and calendars. The falls drops 50 feet into a clear, unpolluted stream that supports a variety of fish and other wildlife, including large snapping turtles. Only a few marks in the stone indicate the site of the old mill; its millstones are displayed next to a new bridge that crosses the stream just above the falls.

PHOTOGRAPHER *I rephotographed this view of Cedar Falls in autumn. The inset is one of many stock images that I have taken of the falls in early spring, when the volume of water is much greater.*

Ohio University Alumni Gate, Athens, circa 1935 (Athens County)

When the Ohio Company made its original land purchase in 1787, one of its conditions was to set aside two townships for higher education. To fulfill the mandate, Athens and Alexander townships were chosen and surveyed in 1795, with the first settlers arriving there in 1797. Ohio University, the first institution of higher learning in the Northwest Territory, was chartered in 1804 and awarded its first diplomas in 1815. The Alumni Gate was erected in 1915 to commemorate the centennial of the university's first graduation.

The corner of Union and Court Streets is the boundary between town and gown in Athens. Beyond the Alumni Gate lies the campus green, the heart of Ohio University. Just to the left of the gate is the 1893 Civil War memorial. The building to the right is Chubb Hall, which was built in 1931 to serve as the campus library but is now home to the university's administrative offices.

Court Street, Athens, circa 1940 (Athens County)

Athens remains a small town, tucked into the hills along the Hocking River. By the 1940s, Court Street was lined with businesses and restaurants serving both students and residents. The tower at left is the clock tower of the Athens County Courthouse, completed in 1880. The courthouse clock was originally installed at Athens City Hall, but was moved to the courthouse in 1917. The large building in front of the courthouse with the prominent roof cornice is the Masonic Hall.

After 60 years, the most obvious changes are the stoplights and the names of the businesses, with the neon signs of the local bars and grills replaced by Taco Bell. Even the streetlights, though new, are similar in style to their predecessors.

Athens Lunatic Asylum, 1900 (Athens County)

Though even the name "lunatic asylum" sounds cruel to us today, the movement behind the construction of what later became the Athens Mental Health Center was compassionate: the acceptance of public responsibility for the mentally ill. The asylum opened in 1874 in the large double-towered building just right of center, which was built of brick made on the grounds. It served as the main administration building as well as a place for housing patients. As the institution grew, a network of ponds was built at the base of the ridge on which the buildings sat and became a favorite recreation area for the people of Athens. The asylum was a major spur to Athens' growth from 1870 to 1900.

The last patient left the Athens Mental Health Center in 1993. Since then, most of the property has been acquired by Ohio University and is known as The Ridges. The main administrative building, now barely visible above the trees, has been remodeled and is the home of the Kennedy Museum of Art. Years of frequent flooding of Athens and the OU campus motivated the Army Corps of Engineers to remove the scenic lakes in 1969 and reroute the channel of the Hocking River along the base of the ridge. In this photo, the low embankment behind the bicyclist marks the river; a road runs farther back near the treeline.

Canaan Coal Company Store, circa 1915–1920 (Athens County)

One of many southeast Ohio coal companies, the Canaan Coal Company operated a 423-foot-deep shaft mine at Canaanville from 1906 to 1925. Like most mining companies, Canaan Coal ran a company store, a touchy subject in coal country. The companies claimed the stores were simply a service to their employees and that the companies not only made no profit from the stores, but would have preferred not to deal with them. To the miners, the stores were a way for the company to keep its money from being spent elsewhere. Miners were often paid in scrip that could only be used at the company store, and the credit extended by the stores during slow times often meant the miners and their families were perpetually in debt to the company.

The decline of the coal industry left derelict mines, ghost towns, and shuttered store buildings across southeast Ohio. The Canaan Coal store building has fared better than many and currently awaits a new tenant. It appears much the same as it was nearly a century ago, but with a rebuilt porch and the old signage carefully removed.

Ross County Courthouse, Chillicothe, 1885 (Ross County)

Chillicothe was the first and third capital of Ohio, from 1803 until 1810, when the state government moved to Zanesville, and again from 1812 until the legislature moved to Columbus in 1816. Ohio's first statehouse stood on this corner in Chillicothe until it was demolished in 1852 to make way for the new Ross County Courthouse. The tower clock faces were installed in 1856, but the works to run them weren't installed until 11 years later, when the county commissioners also added the bell cupola. The tracks in the intersection at Paint and Main Streets are for horsecars. The sign leaning against the pole just right of center advertises the 27th Annual Ohio State Fair.

The exterior of the courthouse has changed little in the past 120 years, although a careful observer will notice that the black clock face with white numerals is now white with black numerals. The interior has been modified over the years to accommodate changing county offices, including a complete remodeling in 1901 that included the addition of an inlaid mosaic of the Great Seal of the State of Ohio just inside the main entrance.

Adena, 1898 (Ross County)

This sandstone mansion was the centerpiece of Adena, the 2,000-acre estate of Ohio governor and U.S. senator Thomas Worthington. Completed in 1807, the home was designed by Benjamin Henry Latrobe, the architect of the U.S. Capitol. This photo was taken two years after the death of Martha Piatt Reed Worthington, Thomas Worthington's daughter-in-law and the last Worthington to live at Adena. After her death, the house sat empty for several years before being purchased by the Smith family of Chillicothe, who remodeled and redecorated the home and retained ownership until 1946. The insets show Adena's large back garden.

The Smith family gave Adena to the state of Ohio in 1946. The Ohio Historical Society opened the house for tours while carrying out a restoration that was completed in 1953. In 1997, the historical society began research for a second restoration, using new techniques to determine original finishes and decor. The new restoration was completed in 2003.

Ohio River and Floodwall, Portsmouth, circa 1909 (Scioto County)

Sited at the confluence of the Scioto and Ohio Rivers, Portsmouth's history has been dominated by its relationship with the mighty Ohio. The area's original settlement was Alexandria, on the west side of the Scioto. After repeated floods, Alexandria's settlers moved to the higher eastern bank of the river, founding Portsmouth. By 1814, Alexandria was gone, its former citizens snug on high ground.

Alas, not high enough. Portsmouth suffered eight floods between 1832 and 1883. In 1884 and 1907, the river crested at well over 60 feet and caused extensive damage to downtown. In 1908, the city constructed its first floodwall, but in 1913, the river topped the wall not once, but twice. The floodwall was raised, then raised again in 1930, protecting downtown from a river height of up to 62 feet. In 1936, the river rose to within 6 inches of the top of the wall before dropping, and Portsmouth declared itself "flood proof."

Mother Nature had other ideas. In December 1936 and January 1937, heavy rain settled over the Ohio Valley, falling for 22 consecutive days in Portsmouth. It became obvious that the rising river would top the floodwall, and city officials evacuated the city and reluctantly opened the valves that would allow the water to rise slowly through the sewer drains, rather than risk a breach in the floodwall. The swollen river crested at 74.23 feet.

After the 1937 flood, work began on the Portsmouth–New Boston Flood Protection Project, which included a system of dams, reservoirs, flood channels, and dikes as well as a much taller floodwall for the city of Portsmouth. The project was completed in 1950 and protects the city from a river height of up to 77.2 feet. Portsmouth has not been flooded since.

The historical photo looking west shows Portsmouth's first floodwall shortly after it was completed in 1909. The commercial buildings along Front Street look out over the Ohio River, only a matter of feet from the low wall that was their only protection from the river.

Today's floodwall completely blocks the view of Front Street, where many of the old buildings still stand. The interior surfaces of the floodwall are covered with murals depicting Portsmouth's history, helping to relieve the feeling of enclosure behind the high walls (see photo at right). In the background is the Carl D. Perkins Bridge across the Ohio River.

PHOTOGRAPHER *I am still amazed when I think that the floodwaters of 1937 would have reached within 3 feet of the top of the wall in the "now" photo. The car would have been submerged under several feet of water, with only the painted stars on the top of the wall still showing!*

Ohio River and General U. S. Grant Bridge, Portsmouth, 1935 (Scioto County)

This view looking east shows the 1930 floodwall at the left. The woman sitting on the concrete wall seems to be deep in thought as she is photographed from the car in the foreground. The original General U. S. Grant Bridge, completed in 1927, crosses the Ohio in the background.

Again, the current floodwall blocks any view of the city. Looking at this photo, it is hard to imagine the river coming anywhere close to the wall, let alone topping it. The old Grant Bridge was demolished in 2001 and is currently being replaced.

Columbia Theatre, Portsmouth, 1937 (Scioto County)

Only a year after Portsmouth declared itself to be "flood proof," this was the scene on Gallia Street in January 1937. Though it couldn't prevent the massive flood, the city's floodwall at least allowed a more or less orderly evacuation of the city. The decision to open the sewer valves, allowing the floodwater to rise slowly, prevented damage from water rushing into the city over the wall and avoided a break in the wall by alleviating pressure on the river side.

Portsmouth has not flooded since 1937. The Columbia Theatre, which opened in 1910 as a live venue and later added movies to its attractions, survived the flood only to nearly fall victim to decades of neglect. The only vintage theater remaining in Portsmouth, it is now being restored by a local entrepreneur. The Royal Savings and Loan building (now the Royal Lounge) and the office building in the background have also survived both flood and years.

PHOTOGRAPHER *I could not resist the irony of the "one in a million" 1937 photograph when I discovered it in the Southern Ohio Museum's collection. Later that day, as I researched Portsmouth's incredible flood history, I came across a telling and equally ironic prediction made by a weather forecaster in Cincinnati, W. C. Devereaux. Before the 1937 flood, he had predicted the Ohio River would not rise higher than 70 feet at Portsmouth and that there was only "one chance in 1,000 that it could." Sadly, the river ended up rising to a one-in-a-million record of 74.23 feet on January 27, 1937, confounding the experts and leaving most of Portsmouth under 12 feet of water or more.*

Sciotoville Railroad Bridge, Sciotoville, 1916 (Scioto County)

When hired by the Chesapeake & Ohio Railway to design its Ohio River bridge at Sciotoville, Gustav Lindenthal faced some challenges. First, the river measured about 1,600 feet between embankments. Second, the project required two 750-foot navigational clearances, since the normal navigation channel on the Kentucky side of the river switched to the Ohio side during floods. Third, the bridge had to be able to carry two heavily loaded freight trains across the river simultaneously. Lindenthal's solution was a massive, steel, single-truss bridge, shown here from the Kentucky side of the river during its construction. The steel structure was built outward from the central pier. The Ohio side of the bridge (at the left) was built on temporary supports, allowing the Kentucky side to be cantilevered to keep the regular river channel clear.

The finished bridge stands 129 feet high at its center point, which rises 236 feet above the river. The completed structure incorporates 13,200 tons of steel, and its piers required 27,000 cubic yards of concrete and 425 tons of reinforced steel. Ninety years after it was built, the Sciotoville Bridge is still in use and remains the world's longest continuous-truss railroad bridge.

PHOTOGRAPHER *I took this photograph from the Ohio side of the river, looking in almost the opposite direction from the 1916 photograph. The Kentucky side of the river offered no clear view of the bridge.*

Park Central Hotel, Gallipolis, 1937 (Gallia County)

Like all Ohio River cities, Gallipolis has suffered its share of floods. This photo is from the same January 1937 disaster that overtopped Portsmouth's "flood-proof" floodwall. The river crested at a little over 70 feet and poured water into downtown, but fortunately for Gallipolis, the flooding was actually much more severe farther downstream.

Except for the absence of boat traffic in the street, little about the exterior of the Park Central Hotel has changed in the past 70 years. The taxi stand has disappeared, as have some of the surrounding buildings. But the Park Central retains its distinctive sign just under the third-story windows, and the ornate balcony remains. The first-floor storefronts have changed little except for the addition of some awnings, though the old hotel door is considerably modified. Comparing these two photos, it is obvious that the 1937 water depth here was nothing like that downstream in Portsmouth. Only a boat like the one in the photo, with a very shallow keel, could have negotiated the water.

Gallipolis from Fortification Hill, circa 1900 (Gallia County)

This view of Gallipolis shows a sleepy Ohio River town with a couple of sternwheelers at its docks and a ferry landing at the right to provide transportation across the Ohio River to West Virginia. Gallipolis, or "City of the Gauls," was first settled by 500 French royalists fleeing the French Revolution. They purchased land from the Scioto Company, arriving in 1790 to discover that they had been duped—the land in question actually belonged to the Ohio Company. Even after the land swindle had been worked out and the Ohio Company helped build 96 log cabins to shelter the new arrivals, the French had few frontier survival skills. By 1807, there were only about 20 French families that remained in Gallipolis.

Today Gallipolis is a city of about 4,000 people and the county seat of Gallia County. The southeast edge of the city has nearly reached the foot of Fortification Hill, and the northeast edge extends to the Silver Memorial Bridge in the background. This bridge, finished in 1969, replaced the original Silver Bridge built in 1928. That bridge collapsed into the Ohio River in December 1967, killing 46 people.

PHOTOGRAPHER *I was familiar with this great view of Gallipolis and the Ohio River because I had taken a similar shot from Fortification Hill for a magazine assignment several years ago. Consequently, I was quite pleased when I found the 1900s view in a private collection. I took this one from a slightly different angle than the old photograph in order to get a clear view unobstructed by trees. One can still see the dramatic change in the river, however. It is much deeper today, and the bend on the right side is no longer so prominent.*

2nd Avenue, Gallipolis, circa 1951 (Gallia County)

Second Avenue, also known as OH 7, parallels the Ohio River through Gallipolis. In the 1950s it was a thriving commercial strip. The movie theatre at right began life in 1895 as the local opera house and became the Gallipolis Theatre in the early 1900s. When this photo was taken, it was one of two movie theaters on this section of 2nd Avenue. Farther down on the same side of the street (to the right of the car driving toward the camera) is the Lupton Block. Built in 1894, the Lupton Block's unusual arched facade is a Gallipolis landmark.

In the 1990s, the Gallipolis Theatre was restored and reopened as the Ariel Theatre, the home of the Ohio Valley Symphony. In 2004, a gift from benefactor Ann Carson Dater made it possible to purchase the building, which now houses music, dance, and theater classes and hosts live performances of all types. It has been renamed the Ariel Ann Carson Dater Performing Arts Center. The Colony Theatre is now closed. The Lupton Block was restored in 2004 after a disastrous fire heavily damaged the landmark building in 2001.

Northeast Ohio

With easy access via Lake Erie, northeast Ohio was settled early, largely by New Englanders attracted to the lands of the Connecticut Western Reserve—territory once owned by the state of Connecticut—which extended over much of the region. The Western Reserve, which included the area from Lake Erie south to the 41st parallel and west 120 miles from the Pennsylvania border, was one of only two areas not ceded to the federal government by the eastern states when the Northwest Territory was organized. (The other was the Virginia Military District in south Ohio.) Many New Englanders took advantage of the chance to buy land from the Connecticut Land Company and move west into the Ohio Country to settle.

Northeast Ohio lies primarily in the hilly glaciated plateau area. As in other parts of the state, the area's rivers were the first routes inland from the lake, but here they also provided potential power in the form of waterfalls and rapids. The future major cities of northeast Ohio had the advantage of a Lake Erie or Ohio River port for shipping, and the resulting access to raw materials and water power led to the dramatic growth of industry.

Cleveland is northeast Ohio's crown jewel. An industrial powerhouse for decades, Cleveland has spent considerable effort over the past 40 years rejuvenating its downtown and shedding its image as a high-crime, high-pollution urban jungle. The growth of new office buildings around Public Square, the redevelopment of the East 9th Street Pier area, and the construction of major new sports venues downtown have done much to improve visitors' impressions of the Forest City.

South of Cleveland lies Akron, known nationwide as the Rubber City. Once the home of the "big four" tire makers—Goodyear, B.F. Goodrich, Firestone, and General Tire—Akron, too, has worked hard to reinvent itself after the loss of much of its heavy industry, transforming itself into a national center for polymer research.

The cities of Ohio's "Steel Valley," including Youngstown and Steubenville, have suffered due to increased steel imports, but continue to support much of the region's remaining steel industry while working to attract new businesses and industries. Likewise, the pottery industry of northeast Ohio, especially East Liverpool, has diminished but continues to play a role in the area.

But northeast Ohio is not all cities and industry. There is also rolling farmland, especially in the Amish areas of Wayne, Holmes, and Tuscarawas Counties. Cuyahoga Valley National Park—Ohio's only national park—follows the Cuyahoga Valley and the Ohio & Erie Canal, boasting green space and restored historic sites. And Malabar Farm State Park preserves a glimpse of Ohio's agricultural past, while Mohican-Memorial State Forest reclaims land once stripped of its forest cover. These places are just a few reminders of the natural beauty to be found even in this most urban of Ohio's regions.

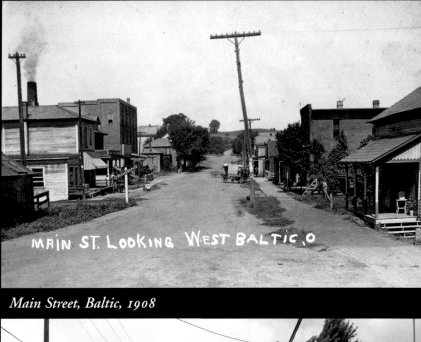

Main Street, Baltic, 1908

Public Square, Cleveland, 1916 (Cuyahoga County)

Testament to the city founders' New England roots, Cleveland's Public Square has always been a central gathering place for Clevelanders. Once one large plot, by 1916 the square had already been divided into quadrants by streets, which allowed for easier streetcar loops. Moving from left to right, some of the distinctive buildings surrounding the square in 1916 include 75 Public Square, with its distinctive contrasting upper story and decorative cornice. This was the original home of the Illuminating Company. First Presbyterian Church, built in 1855, once dominated the square, but by 1916 was dwarfed by its neighbors. The Society for Savings Building (fourth from left) was designed by famous Chicago architects Burnham and Root and featured a large light well and a stained-glass ceiling in the lobby. The massive structure at the center of the photo is the federal courthouse; the Cuyahoga Building (just to the right of the courthouse) was another Burnham and Root design, while its taller neighbor the Williamson Building (directly behind the Soldiers' and Sailors' Monument) was for many years the tallest building in Cleveland. The white stone building across the street from the Williamson Building is the nearly new May Co. department store.

Today the trend around Public Square is definitely vertical, and the old "skyscrapers" seem to shrink into the background. 75 Public Square, the tallest building remaining from the 1916 photo, is now silhouetted against a taller building (left), and even with its new spire, the First Presbyterian Church nearly disappears into the scenery. The Society for Savings Building has been incorporated into the Key Tower, the tallest building in Ohio. The Howard Metzenbaum Federal Courthouse still stands, as does the May Co. building, but the Cuyahoga and Williamson buildings were imploded in 1982 to make way for the BP Tower (center). At right in this photo are the former Higbee's department store building and one wing of Terminal Tower, Cleveland's massive rail terminal.

PHOTOGRAPHER *I took this series of photographs from the Renaissance Cleveland Hotel, which offered the same view of the square as the 1916 panoramic. I faced a serious challenge, though, in capturing the much taller buildings now. I solved the problem by using a very wide-angle lens, making the exposures vertically, and building a platform to extend the camera outside of the window. The only drawback in using the wide-angle lens was that I was not able to match the perspective as well as I would have liked.*

Euclid Avenue at Playhouse Square, circa 1920s (Cuyahoga County)

Although there is no "square" to Playhouse Square, the five theaters located in this small area of Euclid Avenue and East 14th Street were Cleveland's major theater district in the 1920s. Of the five venues, the Hanna and the Ohio hosted the legitimate theater, the Allen was built as a movie house, the Palace featured vaudeville shows, and the State hosted both vaudeville and movies. By 1969, the theaters had deteriorated to the point that the Ohio, the Palace, the State, and the Allen closed within a few months of each other, while the Hanna barely survived.

In 1972, the threatened demolition of the Ohio and the State theaters spurred local preservationists and civic activists to raise funds to save and restore the old theaters. Hard work paid off when the Ohio, the State, and the Palace all reopened during the 1980s, followed by the Allen in 1998. The Playhouse Square Foundation acquired control of the Hanna in 1999. The saving of Playhouse Square is considered one of the great success stories in the revitalization of downtown Cleveland.

East 9th Street Pier, Cleveland, circa 1915–1920 (Cuyahoga County)

Cleveland's East 9th Street Pier opened in 1915. The new pier allowed Great Lakes passenger ships to dock away from the dirt and noise of the industrial docks located farther west around the mouth of the Cuyahoga River. Regular passenger ships came and went from various Great Lakes destinations.

Today the East 9th Street Pier and North Coast Harbor area continues to bustle as the home of the Rock and Roll Hall of Fame and Museum, the Great Lakes Science Center, the steamship *William G. Mather,* the *Goodtime III* cruise ship, and Voinovich Park. The Rock and Roll Hall of Fame's distinctive glass building, designed by I. M. Pei, is a modern Cleveland landmark.

Rocky River Marina, circa 1920 (Cuyahoga County)

Mouth of Rocky River

By 1900, the Rocky River west of Cleveland was the boundary between the towns of Lakewood, situated on its east bank, and Rocky River, its namesake on the west bank. The mouth of the river was a popular place for local yacht owners to tie up their craft. The newly formed Lakewood Yacht Club erected a clubhouse in 1900 consisting of two piano boxes on the east side of the river. By 1920 the club, now The Cleveland Yachting Club, had 1,000 members, a dance hall, a movie theater, tennis and handball courts, a swimming pool, a barber shop, and a restaurant.

After financial disaster and bankruptcy in 1921, the Cleveland Yachting Club reorganized and still occupies its facility on Indian Island. Today the marina is surrounded by the Rocky River Reservation of the Cleveland Metroparks system, which follows the river valley for 13 miles. The deep river valley is a quiet island of green for many of Cleveland's western suburbs.

Ashtabula Harbor, 1926 (Ashtabula County)

Even when this panoramic photo was taken in 1926, Ashtabula Harbor was one of the busiest ports on Lake Erie. The bascule lift bridge (at far right) had been built only a year earlier and operated regularly to allow freighters loaded with coal and iron ore to pass in and out of the harbor. The bridge's large counterweight allowed the 156-foot span to lift using only two 75-horse-power electric motors. During World War II, Ashtabula Harbor received more iron ore than any other port in the world, bound for the steel mills of Youngstown and Pittsburgh.

Ashtabula Harbor is still a busy working port, receiving cargo ships carrying coal, iron ore, limestone, potash, and other commodities from all over the world. The long orange structure at far left on this page is the coal arch, a conveyor belt that carries coal brought to the port by rail across the river, where it is loaded on freighters to be shipped. Today the harbor also sees traffic from pleasure boats. Bridge Street near the harbor has been redeveloped as a shopping area, drawing visitors year-round. The 1925 bascule bridge remains, lifting every 30 minutes to allow ships passage to and from Lake Erie. The bridge was recently wired for decorative lights, which bathe the old bridge in a cobalt blue glow each evening.

PHOTOGRAPHER *The high bluff where I rephoto-graphed the 1926 panorama of the harbor is called Point Park. The Ashtabula Marine Museum is located there, and while browsing through their collection I was thrilled to come across the 1926 framed print of the harbor. I was even more delighted when I walked outside of the museum, print in hand, and was able to view the harbor from the very same spot as the photographer had back in 1926. I was amazed to see the many things that had changed and the few that had not. Notice how a fence still runs at the bottom right-hand side of the picture—although clearly not the same fence as before.*

ASHTABULA HARBOR, O. - APRIL 16-1

Harpersfield Bridge, circa 1915–1920 (Ashtabula County)

The Harpersfield Bridge in Ashtabula County is the longest covered bridge in Ohio, with two 114-foot spans across the Grand River. It was built in 1868 using the Howe truss design. The steel addition was built after the 1913 flood cut a new channel around the north end of the bridge.

The Harpersfield Bridge still carries traffic on CR 154, though with weight limits and in only one direction at a time. It also has a pedestrian walkway, added in the early 1990s. Ashtabula County boasts 16 covered bridges—some historic, some nearly new.

Howard Street Hill, Akron, circa 1900 (Summit County)

In the early 1890s, a trip by horse-drawn wagon up the Howard Street Hill took a half hour and frequently exhausted the horse. When traction streetcars began running up the hill later in the decade, it was a nervous ride: If the power was low, the cars would sometimes stall on the ascent, and if the brakes failed to hold the car on the steep incline, passengers took a harrowing trip backward down the hill. The steep incline on the north bank of the Little Cuyahoga River valley stalled development north of downtown Akron for decades.

The Howard Street Hill is still an interesting drive, but most traffic to Akron's North Hill area is routed across the All America Bridge to the east. The bridge's predecessor, a 16-arch concrete viaduct, opened North Hill to quick development in 1922. The old viaduct deteriorated rapidly due to drainage problems and was notorious for dropping chunks of concrete on houses, sidewalks, and factory yards below. It was demolished in 1978.

Downtown Akron with Quaker Oats, circa 1940s (Summit County)

In the minds of many, Akron will always be the Rubber City because it was once the home of B.F. Goodrich, Firestone, General Tire, and Goodyear Tire and Rubber. But before rubber, Akron was all about oatmeal. In 1856, Ferdinand Schumacher, "The Oatmeal King," founded the German Mills Oatmeal Company. The company merged with two other cereal mills in 1901 and became the American Cereal Company, later renamed the Quaker Oats Company. Quaker's downtown Akron mill operated into the 1950s, contributing the smell of slightly burned oats to Akron's atmosphere.

Today the Quaker Oats mill complex exemplifies the creative reuse of historic buildings. Shops and restaurants fill the old mill buildings, and guests at the Crowne Plaza Quaker Square sleep in the former storage silos. A parking lot and building across the street from the silos now provide parking for the complex, and several of the mill's neighboring industrial buildings still survive in the adjacent lots. The "now" photograph was taken from the FirstMerit Tower.

English Garden, Stan Hywet Hall, circa 1920 (Summit County)

This is the house that rubber built: Stan Hywet Hall was the home of F. A. Seiberling, cofounder of Goodyear, and takes its name from the Old English word for "stone quarry" (pronounced stan HEE-wit). Finished in 1915, the Tudor-style manor sat on more than 1,000 acres, much of it beautifully landscaped gardens. This walled English garden was designed by Ellen Biddle Shipman, one of the country's first well-known female landscape architects.

Today the fully restored walled garden is the only Shipman garden on public view in the United States. Though the plants are larger and more mature, Shipman's precise, symmetrical design is as attractive today as ever. The inset photo at right shows the back of Stan Hywet Hall.

Goodyear Airdock, Akron, circa 1929 (Summit County)

This photo of the Goodyear Airdock was taken not long after its construction in 1929. The huge hangar made Akron a center for the development and construction of dirigibles, including lighter-than-air ships such as the *Akron* in 1931 and the *Macon* in 1934. The scale of the building is staggering: 1,175 feet long, 325 feet wide, and 211 feet tall—a little bigger than eight football fields—with no interior supports. The entire building is mounted on rollers to allow for expansion and contraction due to temperature changes, and on humid days the building sometimes forms its own misty interior "clouds." The inset photos of a dirigible under construction give a better idea of the building's size.

The last dirigibles were built in the airdock in the 1950s. Loral Corporation acquired the Goodyear Aerospace Corporation in 1987, then was itself acquired by Lockheed Martin, which plans to use the facility to build its prototype High Altitude Airship, an unmanned, lighter-than-air vehicle that could be used for surveillance, communications, and weather observation. A fire in May 2006, several months after this shot was taken, damaged an acre of the airdock's rubber skin, but apparently caused no structural damage. Though not open to the public, the airdock is easily visible from US 24 east of Akron.

Central Square, Youngstown, 1930s (Mahoning County)

Youngstown's Central Square in the 1930s was a bustle of automobiles, streetcars, and pedestrians. Four of the city's best-known buildings are shown here. At the far left is a part of what was then called Central Tower, an 18-story Art Deco beauty built in 1929. A bit of the Wick Building, designed by Chicago architects Burnham and Root and finished in 1909, peeks between buildings, with a City Trust & Savings Bank advertisement showing near the roofline. The Union National Bank stands in front of the Wick Building and the Dollar Bank Building is to its right.

Central Square is a calmer place today, with a large area converted to a welcome pedestrian plaza. However, the same four major buildings remain: the Central Tower is basically unaltered, with its Art Deco detailing intact, but has been renamed the Metropolitan Tower; the rear part of the old Union Bank Building has gained a story and the decorative work around its roofline is gone; most changed is the Dollar Bank Building, which was remodeled and clad in granite in the 1970s. And on the Wick Building, the City Trust & Savings advertisement lives on after 70 years.

Steubenville from Moodey's Hill, circa 1897 (Jefferson County)

Along with Youngstown, Steubenville was a part of Ohio's great Steel Valley. The stacks of the LaBelle Iron Works appear at center right in the photo, at the bend of the Ohio River. In 1920, the LaBelle Works merged with two other steel producers, the Whitaker-Glessner Company and the Wheeling Steel & Iron Company, to form the Wheeling Steel Corporation. With Weirton Steel Works just across the river in Weirton, West Virginia, and the Mingo Iron Works (later a part of the Carnegie-Illinois Steel Company) just south of Steubenville in Mingo Junction, Ohio, the area was a steel powerhouse by World War II.

The fate of the steel industry in Steubenville is found in the sesquicentennial and bicentennial histories of the city. The 1947 sesquicentennial book devotes 16 pages to the local steel industry. In 1997, the steel industry not only has no section of its own, it is barely mentioned. This current photo shows a greener and less industrial Steubenville; the former LaBelle Works still stand but are dark. The terraced hillside across the river stands out in the new photo; the hill has been blasted and reshaped in order to widen WV 2, which is visible at its base, and to prevent rockfalls onto the highway.

Court and Market Streets, Steubenville, 1930s (Jefferson County)

This view of downtown Steubenville shows a thriving shopping and business area, with a Montgomery Ward store, Weisberger Freeman Shoes for Men, Richman's, Gray Drugs, and the Olympic Theater. On the right are downtown Steubenville's great landmark buildings, the National Exchange Bank Building (the tall, narrow building at center) and the Sinclair Building (with the Union Bank sign). The Sinclair Building was Steubenville's first skyscraper, in 1914; the National Exchange Building followed in 1922.

As in many Ohio cities, the old commercial buildings have been "improved" over the years. The building that housed Montgomery Ward in the 1930s has been partially reclad in stone panels (right) and its storefronts have been modernized; one of its neighbors has lost its decorative roof cornice. Across the street, the National Exchange Building appears untouched, but the Sinclair Building has acquired a long 1960s-vintage awning connecting it to its neighbor.

North Street Fire Station, Steubenville (Jefferson County)

In 1909, the Steubenville Fire Department was still horse powered. This photo of the old North Street fire station shows the firefighters of the Reliance Company proudly posing with their horse-drawn fire engine. A few years later, a larger station house was built for the expanding company, now showing off two engines.

The second station house still stands with a few modifications, and Steubenville's present firefighters are no less proud of their firefighting equipment than were their predecessors. Porter Helsel, Johnathan Scott, and Mitchell Humienny were kind enough to pose with their trucks.

1909

undated

East Liverpool and Ohio River
1898 (Columbiana County)

Deposits of high-quality clay near East Liverpool, which lies on the Ohio River at the point where Ohio, West Virginia, and Pennsylvania meet, brought an influx of highly skilled potters from England in the 1830s and 1840s. The city soon found itself nicknamed the "Crockery City," the center of the huge pottery industry of east Ohio. This panoramic view of the city shows a large number of the industry's distinctive "bottle kilns." Several of the potteries were located very near the river, where shipping was convenient.

Today the hills upon which East Liverpool is built remain much the same, but the riverbank has changed dramatically. Much of the city's old waterfront has been reclaimed by the river, along with the potteries that once stood there. According to East Liverpool's Carnegie Library, the potteries came and went with such rapidity, often moving or changing names, that no one really knows how many there were—only that they ranged from 30-kiln factories to single-kiln home businesses. Hall China and Homer Laughlin China Company remain today in the East Liverpool area, but like the kilns in the old photo, most of the city's potteries have long since disappeared.

EAST LIVERPOOL FROM NEWELL

Thompson Block, East Liverpool, circa 1895–1905 (Columbiana County)

This photo of the Thompson Block at 6th and Diamond shows four bottle kilns in the background, tucked behind a row of elaborately ornate commercial buildings. The *Sentinel*, the Civil War statue in the Diamond (the triangular area that serves as a public "square"), was erected in 1890.

Only a couple of the old buildings still stand and, typically, they've lost some of those whimsical decorative touches over the years. The turret on the corner building looks a bit naked without its

point. The building next door still stands but has had an unmatched fourth story added, minus the attractive cornices that graced the original. As for the statue from the old photo, the *Sentinel* has led a peripatetic life: In 1909, he was moved to the City Park; he later stood in front of the Carnegie Library; and in 1942 he was finally moved to Riverview Cemetery, where he still stands, facing down the Confederacy.

5th Street, East Liverpool (Columbiana County)

Though not precisely the same, these views up 5th Street from the steps of the East Liverpool post office show the block's gradual transformations over about 30 years. The older photo is probably from the 1910s. Note the drugstore building on the corner and the Moore's Furniture and Carpets advertisement. The second photo is probably from the late 1930s or early 1940s. Most of the buildings remain, but the former drugstore is now faced with brick and the large building in the right background of the previous photos is gone. The Dollar Savings Bank sign is gone and the Moore's sign has been replaced.

Even now, the scene is still recognizable as that same street corner. The old drugstore's entrance has now been moved from the corner of the building to the side, and the trolley wires that webbed the previous two photos are gone. In yet another testament to the staying power of painted advertisements, parts of both versions of the Moore's Furniture sign are still visible at left.

PHOTOGRAPHER *Determining my location and vantage point for this pair of old images was a mere matter of minutes (instead of hours, as was the case for the panoramic view of East Liverpool, pp. 64–65). As I was searching through the archives of the Museum of Ceramics, I came across a series of three photographs (two of which are used here) that were obviously taken from the same location, but some 20 to 30 years apart. When I asked about them, it was quickly pointed out that they were probably taken from just outside the very building we stood in. We stepped outside on the elevated entranceway and, to my amazement, I found I was standing in the very same spot from which they had originally been taken. The elevated entranceway serves as a great vantage point, both now, as the Museum of Ceramics, and then, when it was the East Liverpool post office.*

circa 1910s

circa 1930s

Brandywine Falls, undated (Summit County)

An example of northeast Ohio's abundant water power, Brandywine Falls supported a bustling village in the early 1800s, consisting of a sawmill, the gristmill shown here, a woolen mill, a distillery, a school, a store, a post office, and a number of homes. In 1848, James Wallace, whose father built many of the original mills, constructed a fine Greek Revival house north of the falls. Ironically, the canal system and railroads that stimulated the growth of the state spelled doom for Brandywine Village, as it brought competition from new commercial centers. By 1870, the village was effectively a ghost town.

Today little is left of Brandywine Village. The stone foundation of the old gristmill still remains under the trees at right, capped by concrete block added in the 1920s by William Hale, who housed his electrical supply company in the building. Hale gave up his attempt to revive Brandywine Village after the mill was struck by lightning and burned—twice. One house still stands from the village proper after three others were demolished to make way for I-271, and James Wallace's Greek Revival home remains as the Inn at Brandywine Falls.

Lanterman's Mill, 1928 (Mahoning County)

When German Lanterman opened his gristmill in the Mill Creek valley in 1846, it was already the third mill to use the site. Lanterman's three sets of water-powered grinding stones turned out flour until 1888, when the introduction of less-costly roller mills made it too expensive to continue operations. After its sale to Mill Creek Park in 1892, the mill building was used for a number of purposes, including a bath house for the swimming hole below the falls, a dance hall, and even a boat repair and storage facility.

In 1933, part of the first floor of the mill was converted into a nature museum for Mill Creek Park. In 1972, it became the park's historical museum. It has since undergone a complete structural facelift and restoration of the antique mill machinery, including many parts that had to be painstakingly hand-made, and a reproduction of the water wheel that was constructed off-site, then taken apart and reconstructed at the mill.

Alexander/Wilson Feed Mill, 1890 (Cuyahoga County)

The Alexander Mill was built at Lock 37 on the Ohio & Erie Canal in 1852–1853. It was powered by a horizontal turbine run by water from the canal. The last canal boat to pass by the old mill did so in 1913, the year that the great flood destroyed much of the Ohio & Erie from Cleveland to Portsmouth. The mill was later purchased by the Wilson family. The canal remained the mill's power source until 1969.

Today the Wilson Mill stands in Cuyahoga Valley National Park, though the earlier view is now blocked by an unattractive storage building. Still owned by the Wilson family, the mill now produces animal feed using electric grinders. The mill can be seen from another angle along the Towpath Trail, which runs along the opposite side of the old canal channel (inset photo).

Mustill Store, Ohio & Erie Canal at Akron, circa 1860s (Summit County)

The location of Akron was no accident. When Simon Perkins, a commissioner of the Ohio & Erie Canal, founded the town, he sited it at the high point of the canal, where the necessity of clearing a series of locks would give canal traffic a reason to linger and conduct business. Locks 10–16, called the Cascade Locks, descended to the north of Akron. The Mustill Store at Lock 15 was probably built in the 1850s. Three generations of Mustills operated the store until the late 1880s.

The entire Cascade Locks area was placed on the National Register of Historic Places in 1992. The restoration of the Mustill Store into a visitor and educational center is a first step toward developing an educational park in what was Akron's first industrial valley. Using the Cascade Race that ran parallel to the canal bed from the Little Cuyahoga River for power and the canal for transportation, the area supported an iron foundry, a furniture factory, a distillery, several gristmills, and two rubber plants within a half mile of the canal. The rehabilitation of the Mustill House and Store was a four-way partnership between the Cascade Locks Park Association; Metro Parks, serving Summit County; the city of Akron; and the National Park Service. The people shown in the photo are representatives of the partnering organizations.

Magnolia Flouring Mill, circa 1900 (Stark County)

Built in 1834 by Richard Elson, the Magnolia Flouring Mill benefited greatly from the nineteenth century's two great modes of transportation: canals and railroads. Not only was the mill situated on the Sandy & Beaver Canal (a feeder of the Ohio & Erie), but the Magnolia town railroad station was located directly behind it. The mill was water powered until the 1940s, and its waterwheel still stands in the basement. Magnolia Mill produced white flour until the 1960s, when it began making animal feed.

In the fall of 2005, Richard Elson's great-great-grandson, Augustus Elson II, sold the historic property to the Stark County Park District along with 12.79 acres, including a section of the Sandy & Beaver Canal and its water rights. The park district plans to continue to run the mill and use it as an educational tool.

Main Street, Millersburg, 1911 (Holmes County)

As the seat of Holmes County, Millersburg lies in one of the most rural areas of northeast Ohio. Home to a large population of Amish, Holmes County is, even today, primarily farmland. This 1911 view of the commercial district of Main Street appears nearly deserted, with only a few horses and buggies patiently awaiting their owners. The tallest building, at center left, is the Hotel Millersburg.

The main mode of transportation has changed, but Millersburg's Main Street is still much as it was nearly a century ago. A couple of buildings at center right have been replaced and some decorative finials have been shed, but the Hotel Millersburg looks very much the same as it did in 1911. Parked cars replace the buggies here, but horses and buggies are still a common sight on the streets of Amish country.

Zoar Hotel, 1892 (Tuscarawas County)

Ohio has hosted many religious communities, including the Moravian settlement at Schoenbrunn, the Mormons at Kirtland, Shakers at Shaker Heights and Watervliet, and even a Fourierist outpost, called a phalanx, at Utopia. One of the most successful settlements was founded in 1817 by German Separatists at Zoar. The village was a nearly self-sufficient communal society where men and women worked side by side in the fields and shops. Zoar also became a popular tourist destination for the Germans of Cleveland. The original Zoar Hotel (with tower, at left) was built in 1833, with the expanded structure at right added in 1889.

Both the growing wealth of the Separatists and the loss of their original leader, Joseph Bimeler, contributed to the dissolution of the Society of Separatists of Zoar in 1898. Assets were auctioned and the proceeds divided among members. Today many of Zoar Village's original buildings still stand, a number privately owned. Others are owned by the Ohio Historical Society, including the original hotel building. The addition was demolished years ago.

Zoar School, undated (Tuscarawas County)

Lawrence Township ran the school system, but the Zoarites provided their own building and were allowed to set their own rules on the condition that non-Society children in the area could also go to classes there. Until 1874, only German was taught, but later English also entered the curriculum. This building, the second schoolhouse, was built in 1868.

After the Separatists dissolved their society, the school remained under lease to the township for some time. In 1967, Zoar's sesquicentennial year, the Zoar Community Association was formed. The ZCA's first project was to restore the old school, which had been returned to the village and remained empty since 1953. The building is now used as a community center.

Big House, Malabar Farm, circa early 1950s (Richland County)

Pulitzer Prize–winning writer and conservationist Louis Bromfield was a leader in the development of sustainable farming techniques in the 1940s and raised chickens, goats, and beef cattle as well as corn, hay, oats, and wheat on his 800-plus acres at Malabar Farm. The 32-room Big House was designed to look as if it had been added on to over the years. The house's most famous moment was the wedding of Bromfield's friends Humphrey Bogart and Lauren Bacall on May 21, 1945. Sources in the Ohio Department of Natural Resources identify the woman in this photo as Bromfield's wife, Mary; three of his beloved boxers stand at left. Bromfield himself does not appear.

In his book *Pleasant Valley,* Bromfield mused that "Perhaps one day [the Big House] will belong to the state together with the hills, valleys and woods of Malabar Farm." His wish came true in 1972 when the state of Ohio accepted the deed to the farm, which is today a state park. The state has preserved Bromfield's farming methods and Malabar remains a working farm. The Big House stands just as Bromfield left it in 1956. Continuing Bromfield's sustainable farming legacy, the park is opening a new education center where visitors can learn about the history of the farm and experience agricultural life. Pictured above, from left to right, are Lisa Durham, Karla Abele, Louis Andres, and Lori Fraizer.

Memorial Forest Shrine, Mohican-Memorial State Forest, circa 1945–1955 (Ashland County)

By the end of the Civil War, Ohio had been stripped of nearly all its forest cover. The Mohican-Memorial State Forest was originally cleared for agriculture, but after years of farming, the land quality eroded and fertility dropped. In 1928, the state began acquiring this abandoned farmland and the Civilian Conservation Corps began mass plantings of mixed pine species in the 1930s. This photo was taken in the late 1940s or early 1950s when the new plantings around the Memorial Shrine were only about 10 to 15 years old.

What a difference 50 years makes! Alongside the stands of pine planted by the CCC, native hardwoods have begun to fill in unplanted areas. Mohican-Memorial State Forest is also now one of three Ohio sites where the Division of Forestry has begun planting American elms bred to be resistant to Dutch elm disease, which nearly wiped out elms in the United States after 1930. At their low point in 1910, forested areas covered only 10 percent of the state—now they cover 30 percent.

Southwest Ohio

Except for a tiny sliver of the plateau region at the far southeast edge, the counties of southwest Ohio lie in the Till Plains, a rich region of gently rolling hills and fertile topsoil. The land is crisscrossed by the Great and Little Miami Rivers and their tributaries, which drain into the mighty Ohio in the southwest corner of the state. A welcome source of transportation, water, and power, the Miami watershed has also had its dark moments, such as the great flood of 1913, which killed 300–350 people in the Miami Valley alone and destroyed large parts of Dayton and other river cities. Though the flood was a statewide disaster, the Miami Valley was so hard-hit by the floodwaters that in the late 1910s its citizens embarked on one of the largest flood-control projects ever undertaken, constructing a system of dry dams and levees that still stand—and still do their job admirably.

Cincinnati, the Queen City of the West, anchors the state's southwest corner. Famous at various times for its Ohio River port, its packing industry, its breweries, and occasionally its sheer orneriness, Cincinnati is the metropolitan center for not only southwest Ohio, but large parts of Indiana and Kentucky.

Dayton, near the center of the region, is best known as the home of aviation pioneers Wilbur and Orville Wright and the original home of the National Cash Register Company, which revolutionized the business world with its mechanical cash registers.

Springfield, located northeast of Dayton, supported such industrial powers as Champion Reaper, Mast, Foos & Co., Buffalo Springfield Roller Co., Robbins & Myers, and publishing giant Crowell-Collier. Though the great factories are now largely gone, the city's rich past still shows in its historic buildings and parks.

Once mostly agricultural, southwest Ohio has lost many of its corn and soybean fields to sprawling suburban development, especially along the bustling Cincinnati/Dayton/Springfield corridors of I-75 and I-70. But outside the large cities, crops still thrive and life goes on in small towns, often in homes and buildings that have stood for a century or more.

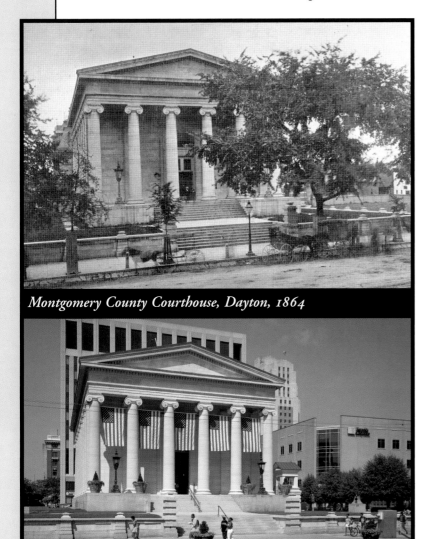

Montgomery County Courthouse, Dayton, 1864

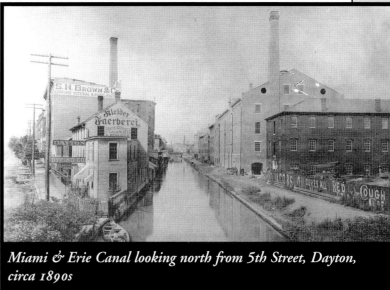

Miami & Erie Canal looking north from 5th Street, Dayton, circa 1890s

Cincinnati from the John A. Roebling Suspension Bridge, 1866 (Hamilton County)

This panoramic shot of Cincinnati was taken from the south tower of the John A. Roebling Suspension Bridge in 1866. The hills—or, rather, glacial plateaus—upon which the city was built are visible, as is the busy riverfront. The Miami & Erie Canal "locked down" to the river at the far right.

    Designed by John A. Roebling, the 1,000-foot bridge (still without a deck here) opened to pedestrian traffic in December 1866 with a toll of a penny per person. This was the longest suspension bridge in the world until the opening of Roebling's Brooklyn Bridge in 1883. The Roebling Suspension Bridge was the only highway span on the Ohio River to remain open during the devastating 1937 flood. The original oak-and-steel bridge deck was replaced in 1896, when a second set of cables was added to support a wider steel-truss deck. Though the old bridge no longer carries streetcar and bus traffic, it remains the busiest of Cincinnati's

non-expressway bridges. Look at the bottom of the bridge pier at center and notice the change in the water level in the Ohio River. This is due partly to heavy rains and flooding in the weeks before this photo was taken, but the Ohio's water level has risen noticeably in the past century due to both natural and man-made changes.

PHOTOGRAPHER *Thanks go to the Kentucky Transportation Cabinet for granting me access to the top of the bridge on the Kentucky side and allowing me to take my four photographs and recreate this fantastic panoramic view of Cincinnati, just as the photographer did back in 1866.*

Cincinnati Union Terminal
circa early 1940s (Hamilton County)

Cincinnati's Art Deco masterpiece, Union Terminal, opened in 1933, consolidating the chaos of seven rail lines and five rail stations into one grand structure. The east facade, shown here, is a 10-story arched structure of limestone and glass, set off by an illuminated fountain, cascades, and a reflecting pool. Two bas-reliefs representing Commerce and Transportation greet visitors at the main doors. When it opened, Union Terminal was the largest half-dome building in the world, a title it held until the opening of the Sydney Opera House in 1973. It remains the largest in the western hemisphere.

Regular train service to Union Terminal ended in 1972. In the early 1980s, the main building was redeveloped as a shopping center, but the venture was not successful. In 1986, the voters of Hamilton County approved a $33 million bond issue to restore the building, which reopened in 1990 as the Cincinnati Museum Center. Today it houses the Cincinnati Historical Museum and Library, the Cincinnati Museum of Natural History & Science, the Children's Museum of Cincinnati, and the Robert D. Lindner Family OMNIMAX® Theater. In recent years, limited train service has returned as well, with a stop on Amtrak's Washington, D.C.–Chicago route.

Miami & Erie Canal/Central Parkway, Cincinnati, circa 1910s (Hamilton County)

Unlike the Ohio & Erie Canal in the eastern half of Ohio, the Miami & Erie Canal wasn't conceived from the start as a route from Lake Erie to the Ohio River. The initial sections of the canal connected Middletown and Cincinnati in 1828, with the northern reaches of the canal added later. The use of canals hit its peak around the 1850s, then slacked off, largely due to competition from railroads. By the 1880s, the canal through Cincinnati was being called a "foully-smelling and miasma-breeding" cesspool, polluted by industrial waste, garbage, and dead animals, and became an actual health hazard in some areas.

Like many Ohio canal cities, Cincinnati converted its canal bed to a street bed. But there's more than meets the eye to this stretch of Central Parkway looking west from Race Street. Underneath it lies a section of Cincinnati's greatest public transportation boondoggle, the infamous Cincinnati Subway. Proposed in 1884 as one way to make use of the already-excavated canal ditch, construction of the subway began in 1920 but sputtered to a halt in 1927 when voters refused to spend any more money on it. Several underground tunnels and stations remain, including the Race Street station, and lack only finishing work—and trains.

A Sunday Afternoon in Cincinnati's Eden Park, 1900 (Hamilton County)

In 1869, the City of Cincinnati leased a large tract of land from Joseph Longworth on which to locate the new city waterworks. Joseph's father, Nicholas, a somewhat eccentric attorney, had become wealthy in the early 1800s by accepting parcels of land as payment for his legal services. The tract the city leased (and later bought) had once been Nicholas' "Garden of Eden," his vineyard, which was the beginning of a long-lived wine industry in Cincinnati. Ironically, Nicholas had offered the city 300 acres, including the Garden of Eden, at below-market prices in the 1840s and 1850s; the city paid Joseph 14 times as much as the land would have cost if they had accepted Nicholas' original offer. The Romanesque turret at the top of this photo was a water tower. The waterworks and the surrounding land later became the core of Eden Park.

The Romanesque water tower is now a communications tower and remains one of the city's most distinctive and recognized structures. Eden Park now includes the Krohn Conservatory, the Cincinnati Museum of Art, and numerous monuments, memorial groves, and recreational structures.

PHOTOGRAPHER *I took this photograph in early spring before the trees leafed out so that you could still see the tower. Even so, the greenery nearly obscures it from view. This is just one example of the increase in trees throughout the state.*

Ohio River from Eden Park, circa 1900 (Hamilton County)

This photo appears to be from around the turn of the twentieth century. When it was taken, the Cincinnati riverfront was crowded right down to the waterline and the river saw considerable water traffic, with several large steamboats tied up on the Ohio side (center left).

Today the shapes of the Ohio and Kentucky hills remain unchanged but are more wooded. The river's shoreline has altered considerably over the years due to flooding and a rise in water level, doing away with the tangle of buildings. Though the river still carries significant commercial traffic, none is evident here. The river is still and serene at sunrise.

Miami & Erie Canal Looking North from Green Street, Dayton, circa 1900 (Montgomery County)

This shot of the Miami & Erie Canal shows it splitting at the armory building, with the main channel passing to its left. The man standing in the water illustrates its shallowness; the flat-bottomed canal boats did not require a great deal of depth. Note the railroad bridge in the background at left, a part of a newer mode of transportation that would spell the end of the canals.

Patterson Boulevard has replaced the canal at the left of the armory, and a parking lot is now off to the right. Note the difference in the ground level around the building after the canal was filled in: Most of the lower story of the armory is now underground and, of course, the sloping bank where the original photographer stood is now gone, making it impossible to take a photo from that exact vantage point. The railroad bridge was replaced by a multiple-track concrete overpass that once led to Dayton's Union Station, which in its turn was overshadowed and made obsolete by automobile transportation.

Memorial Hall, Dayton, 1922 (Montgomery County)

Since its dedication in 1910, Dayton's Memorial Hall has hosted everything from high school graduations and performances of *Hair* to auto shows and Tuesday-night wrestling. The hall was built in memory of the dead of the War of 1812, the Civil War, and the Spanish-American War. This photo was taken by Dayton attorney Albert Kern, who was instrumental in the building of Memorial Hall and in acquiring the cannon in the photo, visible at the lower center, to the right of the front staircase. Kern was also an avid amateur photographer who recorded much of the city and surrounding countryside during the early twentieth century.

Sometime after the 1922 photo, Memorial Hall acquired the statue of a World War I doughboy, which guards the entrance with fixed bayonet and has become something of a Dayton icon. With a variety of new downtown arts venues available today, Memorial Hall is mostly used for meetings, banquets, and receptions.

Wright Brothers Flight at Huffman Prairie, 1905 (Montgomery County)

Though Dayton bicycle makers Orville and Wilbur Wright made their first successful powered flight at Kitty Hawk, North Carolina, they did much of their later testing at Huffman Prairie, just east of Dayton. This photo is one of 12 shots taken on September 29, 1905, during the 41st flight of the 1905 Wright Flyer III. Piloted by Orville Wright, the Flyer made 14 circles of the field, a total of 12 miles, in just under 20 minutes.

One hundred years after Flight 41, the Dayton Aviation Heritage National Historical Park commemorated the flight with a celebration entitled "Centennial of Practical Flight, October 5th 1905–2005." Mark Dusenberry built a replica of the 1905 Wright Flyer III and recreated this flight. The 1905 Wright Flyer III was the first airplane to successfully turn and fly for a duration exceeding 30 minutes and is considered the world's first "practical" airplane. Pictured above is a flyover of a slightly later model Wright Flyer, which also participated in the celebration. Modern-day military planes and vehicles make an appropriate backdrop for the tiny Flyer.

Englewood Dam, 1929 (Montgomery County)

After the great flood of 1913 destroyed a large part of the city of Dayton, local residents and businessmen raised more than $2 million to finance flood-control measures for the Miami Valley. The result was the Miami Conservancy District, a regional organization that dredged river channels, built miles of river levees, and constructed five great dams—Lockington, Huffman, Englewood, Taylorsville, and Germantown—to control storm water. Engineer Arthur Morgan's revolutionary dry dams use no mechanical or moving parts. Rather, they trap excess water in retarding basins, as seen on the north side of the dam in this photo, then release it slowly downstream at its normal rate of flow. When not filled with water, the basins were intended to be used as parks.

The Miami Valley flood controls have worked admirably over the past 80 years, with no significant flooding in Dayton since the project was completed. The dams require minimal maintenance—regular inspection of the earthen dams and occasional repairs to the concrete spillways—and provide significant green space. Today the reserves around the dams are managed by the Dayton MetroParks system and are popular recreation areas.

Crowell-Collier Publishing, Springfield, circa 1930s (Clark County)

Springfield in the 1930s was one of Ohio's industrial centers, the home of firms such as Warder, Buffalo Springfield Roller Co., Mitchell & Co. (a forerunner of International Harvester), Robbins & Myers, Mast, Foos & Co., and others. It was also the home of the manufacturing plant for magazine powerhouse Crowell-Collier Publishing Company. Formed after P. F. Collier & Son was bought by Crowell Publishing Company in 1919, Crowell-Collier was most famous for publishing *Collier's Weekly Magazine*, *The American*, and *Collier's Encyclopedia*. Its massive Springfield plant opened in 1924 and featured its own railroad spur into a tunnel at the center of the building.

Essentially unused for decades, the Crowell-Collier building suffered heavy damage in a 1999 fire. The building's owners were ordered to perform repairs to stabilize the massive building after the fire. It still stands, nearly empty and named to the Ohio Preservation Alliance's "Endangered Ohio Sites" list. Many of the industries that built Springfield are gone today, their plants having been demolished. The evidence of their prosperity remains in the city's fine homes, beautiful parks, and enormous fraternal homes, built to take advantage of Springfield's extensive rail connections and central location.

Bushnell House, Springfield, 1927 (Clark County)

Construction of Bushnell House, the residence of Springfield industrialist and future Ohio governor Asa S. Bushnell, began in 1888. As president of Warder, Bushnell and Glessner Company, now known as International Truck & Engine Corporation, Bushnell could afford to construct a house befitting his status in Springfield. Built in the Richardson Romanesque style, the home's exterior featured grouped windows, contrasting stonework, and large arches, while the interior was opulent, with elaborately carved woodwork, ornate fireplaces, and large chandeliers.

Undertaker Austin Richards bought Bushnell House from later owners the Prout family in 1939. After three years of renovation, the home opened as the Richards Memorial Home, today renamed Richards, Raff & Dunbar. The house continues to be an eye-catcher on East High Street, a standout on a street of many large historic homes.

Rankin House, Ripley, undated (Brown County)

John Rankin was a Presbyterian minister and a dedicated abolitionist, and his home, high on a bluff above the Ohio River, was a well-known first stop on the Underground Railroad. Escaping slaves crossing the river from Kentucky climbed a long stairway from the river to receive food and clothing from Rankin and his family and neighbors before moving north. It is said that Harriet Beecher Stowe used one of Rankin's stories about a slave who carried her baby across the frozen Ohio River as the basis for an incident in *Uncle Tom's Cabin.*

Today Rankin House is an Ohio Historical Society site. In August 2005, $25,000 in federal funding was approved to support an archaeological survey of the Rankin House site. Researchers hope to locate, among other things, the foundations of the Rankins' barn and the wooden addition at the left side of the house in the old photo. The inset photo gives a good indication of why this modest house became such a well-known part of the Underground Railroad; a lamp in the window could clearly be seen along a large part of the Kentucky side of the river.

Commercial Square, Georgetown, circa 1890s (Brown County)

Commercial Square in Georgetown has changed little since this photo was taken around the end of the 1800s. As in many Ohio county seats, the streets around the courthouse square were made wide to accommodate market traffic and horse-and-buggy parking. The seat of Brown County, Georgetown is best known as the birthplace and childhood home of Ulysses S. Grant, one of eight presidents to hail from Ohio.

The biggest change in this scene over the past century has been the switch from hay-burning to gasoline-burning transportation. A few of the older buildings in the background are gone, and adding space for diagonal parking along the street has pushed back the courthouse lawn a bit at the right. Changing the location of the corner made it a challenge to align the new shot with the old.

PHOTOGRAPHER *The old photograph was taken from the second story of a building that is no longer there. I attempted to take the new photograph from my ladder, which experience had taught me to bring along throughout this project. Luckily, as I precariously struggled to get high enough for the shot, a gentleman from the local cycle shop saw my predicament and was kind enough to offer me the use of his taller, 16-foot aluminum ladder.*

Bailey House, Georgetown, circa 1890s (Brown County)

George Bailey, the Georgetown physician who built Bailey House in 1832, was an acquaintance of Jesse Grant, the father of Civil War general and U.S. president Ulysses S. Grant. The story goes that Grant learned Bailey's son Bart was leaving West Point; Grant quickly applied to fill the vacancy and the rest, as they say, is history. This photo was taken around the turn of the twentieth century and shows a wing at left that replaced an original log structure next to the house.

In 1876, Bailey House was purchased by attorney Jesse Thompson. Today the home is a bed-and-breakfast, operated by Jesse Thompson's great-granddaughter and her husband. The house was listed on the National Register of Historic Places in 1976.

Mariemont, 1926 (Hamilton County)

Mary Muhlenberg Emery, founder of Mariemont (pronounced MARY-mont), was convinced that the congestion and substandard housing found in most cities was the result of poor city planning. Mrs. Emery worked with architect John Nolen to develop a planned community for "people of modest means." Ground was broken for the first buildings in 1923. Among Mariemont's innovations were garages designed for automobiles, not horses and carriages. The streetscape above shows the half-timbered Tudor style of the homes and commercial buildings. The large corner building was Mariemont's sales and rental office.

Mariemont was managed by the Mariemont Company and its successor, the Thomas J. Emery Memorial Foundation, until it was incorporated as a village under Ohio law in 1941. Mrs. Emery's visionary community continues to be a highly desirable place to live after 80 years, with most of the original downtown intact and some of the original housing stock still in use. Children of longtime residents often return to raise their families here. The former rental office is now the Best Western Mariemont Inn.

Spring Grove Lake, 1940s (Hamilton County)

Sometimes a beautiful park is much more than just a park. When it opened in 1845, Spring Grove Cemetery was the first in Ohio to embrace a trend toward rural, parklike cemeteries. The Cincinnati Horticultural Society began planning for Spring Grove in the 1830s during a cholera epidemic that brought to the city's attention the crowded, often unkempt city graveyards. The new cemetery, with its lush plantings and walking paths, became an attractive place to stroll and picnic as well as visit the graves of family members.

Today Spring Grove is as well-known for its vibrant landscape, handsome architecture, and champion trees as for its famous occupants, who include Civil War general Joseph Hooker, U.S. Secretary of the Treasury and U.S. Supreme Court Chief Justice Salmon Chase, and 33 Revolutionary War soldiers. The trees and plants around the lake appear to have been thinned and tamed somewhat over the years, opening up the views beyond the lake.

Spring Grove Chapel, 1940s (Hamilton County)

Spring Grove's Romanesque or Norman chapel was completed in 1880. The exterior is of rough-hewn sandstone and limestone and features imported stained-glass windows, while the interior is intricately arched.

PHOTOGRAPHER *I came down in early spring to rephotograph the 1940s picture. I have made it a tradition to visit this incredible cemetery and arboretum in the spring because of its incomparable natural beauty and therefore knew the best time to match the blooms in the old photograph. As I took the picture, I reflected on the stunning magnolia blossoms —over the last 60 years, these same trees have brought pleasure and solace to countless people and are as beautiful now as they were then.*

Seven Caves, circa 1950s–1970s (Highland County)

Eastern Highland County is the meeting place of four geographical areas: the Till Plains, the unglaciated plateau of southeast Ohio, the glaciated plateau, and a small triangle of the Lexington Plain—bluegrass country—that extends up from Kentucky. Rivers and streams have eroded the local dolomite limestone into striking canyons and caves that support dozens of rare plants. This mid-twentieth-century photo shows an iron bridge spanning the narrow canyon.

Seven Caves was a privately owned recreation and camping destination after it was purchased by Clyde Chaney in 1928. In 2006, ownership passed to the Highlands Nature Sanctuary, which plans to change the park's emphasis to education and preservation of the area, protecting its rare plant and animal inhabitants. Those who visit will undoubtedly continue to use the old iron bridge's replacement, which still spans this gorgeous little canyon.

Serpent Mound, 1917 (Adams County)

Serpent Mound is the largest and best-known serpent effigy mound in the United States. Over 1,000 feet long and an average of 3 feet in height, it represents an uncoiling serpent with a huge egg in its mouth, a very large head, or a gigantic eye, according to various interpretations. Serpent Mound was first discovered in modern times by two Chillicothe men during a surveying expedition in 1846. Frederick Ward Putnam of Harvard University's Peabody Museum visited in 1885. Discovering that the mound was gradually being destroyed by farmers' plows, Putnam raised funds to purchase the land, then spent three years excavating and restoring Serpent Mound and two nearby conical mounds. Harvard University turned over the mound and the surrounding land to the Ohio Historical Society in 1901, to be operated as a public park.

Today the Ohio Historical Society maintains a museum and observation tower at Serpent Mound. The mound was long thought to be a remnant of the Adena culture (800 BCE–100 CE), but more recent evidence dates it to the Fort Ancient culture of AD 1000-1550. The site also includes three Adena burial mounds and remnants of a Fort Ancient village near the serpent's coiled tail.

Cascades, Glen Helen, 1910 (Greene County)

Dayton photographer Albert Kern took this photo during a Dayton Camera Club outing at Glen Helen near the village of Yellow Springs, capturing one of his fellow hobbyists at work. Glen Helen also features the Yellow Spring, an iron-rich mineral water spring for which the nearby village was named. In the early years of the twentieth century, there were a number of hotels, spas, and mills in the Glen Helen area, as well as an old stagecoach road and a railroad line.

Nearby Antioch University acquired Glen Helen in the 1920s. Further development of the area was halted, and today the Glen connects with John Bryan State Park and Clifton Gorge to preserve hundreds of acres of cliffs, river gorges, and wooded hills.

PHOTOGRAPHER *I photographed this image from a spot just slightly to the right of where Albert Kern took his 1910 photo, in order to keep the large tree in the foreground from obscuring the cascades. The two smaller trees on the left side of the picture are obviously not the same as those in his shot, but are in a similar location and help visually match up this photo pair.*

The Golden Lamb, Lebanon, early 1900s (Warren County)

The Golden Lamb has operated continuously as a tavern and inn since 1803, hosting luminaries such as the Earl of Derby, later the prime minister of England; De Witt Clinton; and Charles Dickens, who was singularly unimpressed by his inability to obtain brandy at the inn. "We...have nothing to drink but tea and coffee. As they are both very bad, and the water is worse, I ask for brandy; but it is a Temperance Hotel, and spirits are not to be had for love or money," huffed Dickens in *American Notes*. The Golden Lamb has also witnessed the passing of some famous souls, notably Charles Sherman, father of General William Tecumseh Sherman, and Clement Vallandigham, a controversial Civil War–era politician who accidentally shot himself in his room and is said by some to haunt the building.

Today the Golden Lamb, a National Historic Landmark, remains a prominent sight on South Broadway in Lebanon. The old inn still offers overnight accommodations, dining, and the Blackhorse Tavern for those who, like Charles Dickens, desire spirituous beverages during their visit.

Public Square, Troy, circa 1887 (Miami County)

Around 1887, the public square in Troy, the seat of Miami County, featured carefully cultivated trees and an impressive gazebo. The handsome commercial buildings in the background reflect Troy's prosperity, partly a result of its location on the Miami & Erie Canal.

Troy's square is today a large traffic circle (the terror of local driving students), with very similar buildings on both sides. An interesting sidenote: In June 1974, the first retail UPS scanner was installed in a Marsh's supermarket in Troy.

Northwest Ohio

The northwestern section of Ohio was the last to be opened to white settlement, having been mostly set aside for Native peoples in the Treaty of Greenville in 1795. Except for a few whites who pushed in illegally, northwest Ohio was not settled extensively until after the War of 1812, at which point Ohio's Indian tribes were confined to reservations.

In addition to legal restrictions, settlement in northwest Ohio faced a formidable natural obstacle, too: the Great Black Swamp. A nearly impenetrable forest, the swamp was so wet in places that a horse could easily become mired to its chest. Looking across the flat, open fields today, it is hard to imagine that only a century and a half ago, the trees here were so large that settlers used their hollowed-out trunks as temporary homes and barns. Land-hungry farmers cut and burned those trees by hand to get to the the rich soil, which they drained and planted.

An odd bit of evidence remains of the Black Swamp's grip: Driving among the green fields of Mercer, Shelby, and Auglaize Counties, visitors often comment on the number of church spires visible from horizon to horizon. The churches seem incredibly close together to modern eyes—about 3 miles apart. Why? Because when those churches were built, it was nearly impossible to travel more than a mile or two through the swamp to get to church on Sunday.

The largest city in northwest Ohio is, by far, Toledo. In modern times, Toledo has emerged as a glassmaking center and as the home of the Jeep, but historically, it may be best known as the city over which the State of Ohio and the Michigan Territory went to war.

A surveying glitch and congressional vagueness left Ohio's northern border in question when statehood was declared in 1803. Michigan and Ohio were each convinced that Toledo, which lay within the disputed area, was vital to its growth. After some years of dueling surveys, Michigan's territorial governor declared war on Ohio over the issue. The war was short and mostly a comedy of errors by the rival militias. No blood was shed, save for that of a couple of unfortunate mules. The federal government eventually declared that Toledo belonged to Ohio, and in return, Michigan received its mineral-rich Upper Peninsula.

4-H Club Excursion, Sandusky, 1931

Toledo Riverfront, 1912 (Lucas County)

Toledo's port was once thought to be so vital to the growth of Ohio and Michigan that it was worth a declaration of war. Though Michigan survived nicely without it, Toledo is still the largest city in northwest Ohio, thanks in great part to its Lake Erie/Maumee River port access. This 1912 photo shows the steamers *City of Toledo* and *State of New York,* with the stacks of the Toledo Edison steam plant in the background.

The "now" photo was shot from the Martin Luther King, Jr. Memorial Bridge, formerly the Cherry Street Bridge, on the Maumee River. Though Toledo is still very much a working port, in this area most of the old riverfront warehouses are gone, replaced by offices and entertainment and tourist venues. The Toledo Edison plant has lost a stack over the years, and the only other recognizable building—formerly the Ohio Bank Building, now National City Bank—is no longer the standout "skyscraper" it once was.

Maumee River and Cherry Street Bridge, Toledo, 1939 (Lucas County)

When the city of Toledo annexed East Toledo in 1853, the only transportation between the two halves of the city was a ferry across the Maumee. The first Cherry Street Bridge opened in 1865, with a drawbridge to accommodate shipping traffic on the river. This wooden span was replaced by a new iron bridge in 1884 after being damaged by river ice. The iron bridge was half knocked down by a river steamer in 1908 and replaced in 1914 with steel and concrete. When this photo was taken in 1939 (27 years after the 1912 riverfront photo; see p. 107) the Toledo riverfront was still an industrial and warehouse district, with Trinity Episcopal Church nestled among the nondescript buildings.

This recent shot, taken in nearly the opposite direction from the preceding photo pair, shows again the gentrification of Toledo's riverfront. Renamed the Martin Luther King, Jr. Memorial Bridge in 1988, the venerable 1914 structure remains, though it has undergone extensive repairs in recent years after suffering serious damage from overweight truck traffic. Trinity Church still occupies its corner, dwarfed by its neighbors.

PHOTOGRAPHER *I took this same view of the Maumee River from the National City Building, which was the Ohio Bank Building when the earlier photograph was made. I included the ledge of the building in the bottom right corner just as was done before.*

Superior Street, Toledo, 1937 (Lucas County)

This Toledo streetscape has much in common with many Ohio cities in 1937: the F.W. Woolworth store on the corner at left, the rows of automobiles parked along the curbs, the now-unused streetcar tracks in the streets, and the web of electric wires for trackless trolley buses like the one at the center of the photo. These trolleys were quiet and comfortable and could go anywhere an electric wire could be hung, without having to build a network of steel tracks.

Today many of the same buildings stand on Superior Street, but the bustle of shoppers has largely disappeared, along with the Woolworth store and the trolleys, which were replaced statewide with diesel buses in the 1960s. Dayton is the only Ohio city that still uses electric trolleys for mass transit downtown.

Marathon Oil Building, Findlay, circa 1930s (Hancock County)

This impressive structure, a monument to oil and optimism, was the headquarters of the Ohio Oil Company. Founded in Lima, Ohio, in 1887, "The Ohio" became the largest producer in the state, eventually moving to Findlay in 1905, where it erected this new headquarters building in 1929. The company acquired the Marathon product name in 1930 when it purchased the Transcontinental Oil Company. Later it changed its company name to the Marathon Oil Company in 1962.

Marathon Oil became a wholly owned subsidiary of the United States Steel Corporation in 1982 and moved its headquarters to Houston, Texas, in 1990. But it continues to occupy its former Findlay headquarters, expanded over the years, as one of the area's largest employers.

Main Street Looking North from Crawford Street, Findlay, circa 1885 (Hancock County)

The city of Findlay was a major center of the great natural gas and oil boom in northwest Ohio in the late nineteenth century. Natural gas was discovered here as early as 1836 but was regarded mostly as a curiosity until 1884. In the fall of that year, Dr. Charles Osterlen and a group of investors ignored state geologists who pooh-poohed the possibility of finding profitable quantities of gas in the area and drilled a well more than 1,092 feet down, striking the great gas bed of the Trenton limestone formation. The seemingly inexhaustible gas and oil deposits of the Trenton formation made Ohio the nation's leading oil producer by 1896. The investment and industry attracted by oil and abundant natural gas fueled the growth of Findlay for decades.

This postcard shows Findlay's Main Street around 1885, during the early years of the oil boom. The Hancock County Courthouse dome is visible on the left, and the electric arc light at the top center was the latest in street-lighting technology. Perhaps inevitably, Findlay was one of the first American cities to boast gas street lighting (bottom left photo). A history of Hancock County described its effect: "[A] pin in the street, which is 100 feet wide, can be readily picked up, and the finest print can be read as easily as in a parlor in Toledo...."

The streetcar tracks are gone and the street lighting has changed, but many of the buildings remain from the boom years, including the venerable courthouse. If you look closely you can still make out a painted advertisement for the long-gone Leon's Clothing House on the building at center right.

PHOTOGRAPHER *I took this photo slightly to the right of the 1890 photograph location in order to keep some key elements of the courthouse in view. Note that the light is green, which means I was dashing off the street intersection a fraction of a second after I clicked the shutter. The digital thermometer shows how hot it was that day in Findlay.*

Main Street and First Lutheran Church, Findlay, circa 1885 (Hancock County)

This photo was taken from the First Presbyterian Church at the corner of Main and Hardin Streets, looking south down Main. The large church at center is First Lutheran. Dedicated in 1881, this church was well-known for its beautiful stained-glass windows on the north, south, and west sides of the building.

This similar view was shot from the roof of the Marathon Oil building, built in 1929 on the former site of the Presbyterian church. First Lutheran Church still stands at the center of the photo. The original brick and stone structure has been replaced, but the stained-glass windows were salvaged

and reused. Some of the commercial buildings at the right remain, while most nearby residences have been replaced by businesses. Note the large trees that now obscure the background structures.

PHOTOGRAPHER *One of the first features to catch my attention both in the historical photograph and when I went to take the new one was the ornate stained-glass window. My family attended this church when I was a child and I vividly remember passing by the gorgeous window on Sunday mornings.*

Kimmel and Boger Residences, Findlay
circa 1880–1885 (Hancock County)

During the heady years of the oil and gas boom, beautiful residences sprang up along Findlay's Main Street south of downtown, including the Kimmel residence and the Boger house. Notice the large open areas around and behind the houses and what appears to be a small barn to the right of the Boger house. The rail fences were not there for decoration; they were built to keep the neighborhood cattle from wandering into the lawns.

The Boger house has lost a wraparound porch over the years, and the Kimmel home has gained a columned porch across the width of its facade, while losing the rather ornate finial on its turret. But the outstanding difference then and now is the change in what was originally a nearly rural area. Gone are the open fields and lots, replaced by homes and trees beside and behind. Also gone are the cattle fences, since the likelihood of a cow wandering down Main Street is low these days.

Put-in-Bay Harbor and Mystic Isle, late 1940s (Ottawa County)

An unidentified group of explorers sailed among the 20-odd islands in Lake Erie's western basin in 1784. On their charts, they identified one island as "Pudding Bay" because the shape of its harbor reminded them of a pudding bag. That island, now called Put-in-Bay or South Bass Island, gained fame during the War of 1812 as the base from which Oliver Hazard Perry sailed to defeat the British fleet in the Battle of Lake Erie. Perry's note to General William Henry Harrison is familiar to every student of American history: "We have met the enemy, and they are ours, Two ships, two brigs, one schooner and one sloop." The recent view of Put-in-Bay Harbor (opposite) was taken from the top of the Perry's Victory and International Peace Memorial.

PHOTOGRAPHER *This was one of the few times I decided to use an existing photograph of mine and find the old photograph to match it. I knew that this popular vantage point from Perry's Victory and International Peace Memorial had inspired many photographs since it opened to the public in 1915. This one provided a great match of Mystic Isle, with the Jet Express ferry now prominent in the foreground.*

Put-in-Bay Harbor and Perry's Victory and International Peace Memorial, circa 1930s–1940s (Ottawa County)

This postcard illustration of Put-in-Bay Harbor shows some of the beautiful wooden pleasure boats of an earlier era. In the background is Perry's Victory and International Peace Memorial, more commonly called the Perry Monument. Construction of the 352-foot column began 100 years after Oliver Hazard Perry's naval victory in the Battle of Lake Erie in 1813. It opened to the public in 1915 and became a national monument in 1936. The observation deck offers a breathtaking view of Put-in-Bay Harbor and South Bass Island, as seen in the previous photo pair.

The Perry Monument continues to tower over Put-in-Bay Harbor. Although there is much to be said for today's sturdy, more maintenance-free boats, they arguably lack the elegance of the older wooden models.

Miller Boat Dock, Catawba Island, circa 1920s (Ottawa County)

William Miller and Harry Jones went into the ice business in 1905, harvesting block ice from Lake Erie during the winter months and selling it to Put-in-Bay sailors during the summer. Miller also operated a water taxi between the Bass Islands and Catawba Point and was contracted to haul mail from the mainland to the islands. Their dock at Catawba Island became a major transportation link in the mid-1940s, when the Miller family bought out the Catawba Dock Company and began running scheduled ferries from Catawba Point to the islands.

A hundred years after William Miller and Harry Jones started their ice business, the Miller Boat Line dock is the gateway to South Bass Island for thousands of tourists each year. While no longer the only reliable way to get to South Bass, it remains a Bass Islands mainstay.

Marblehead Lighthouse, circa 1890s (Ottawa County)

Marblehead Lighthouse is the oldest continuously operating lighthouse on the Great Lakes. Originally known as the Sandusky Lighthouse, it was built in 1821 of locally quarried limestone. The tower stood 50 feet tall and was lighted by 13 whale-oil wicks.

Marblehead's height was increased by 15 feet in 1897, and its light source has changed from whale oil to kerosene to electricity. Automated in 1958, Marblehead is now operated by the U.S. Coast Guard. The area around the light is maintained as a park by the Ohio Department of Natural Resources, with a museum in the reconstructed keeper's house at left. Through it all, Marblehead Lighthouse has provided guidance to Lake Erie ships for more than 180 years.

Interurban Bridge and Roche de Boeuf, Waterville, circa 1910s (Lucas County)

A testament to the glory days of electric interurban trains, the "Electric Bridge" at Waterville was trumpeted as the largest reinforced concrete railroad bridge in the world when it opened in 1908. The bridge was controversial from the start. One of the middle piers rests on historic Roche de Boeuf, where Indian chiefs Little Turtle, Blue Jacket, and Tarhe the Crane met to plan their strategy against General "Mad" Anthony Wayne in 1794. The interurban company naturally claimed that their bridge could only enhance access to the rock formation and other historic Indian sites.

The Electric Bridge was abandoned in 1937 when the interurban line went out of business. It reopened briefly in 1941 as a temporary automobile bridge, but today is unused and deteriorating. The National Park Service placed the bridge on its National Register of Historic Places in 1972.

Lakeside Dock and Beach House, circa 1920 (Ottawa County)

The community of Lakeside began in 1873 as a revival site founded by a group of Methodist preachers. Later used as a training ground for Sunday school teachers, Lakeside became a part of the Chautauqua movement in the 1890s and hosted educational and cultural programs as well as famous speakers. The beach house and docks are shown here around 1920, when many guests arrived via steamboats like the *Arrow,* docked at left.

Though no longer made of wood, the docks remain much the same. The original beach house was demolished in 1961 and replaced with a completely different structure. The current pavilion was erected in 1988 and recalls the style of the original. By adapting to modern expectations, Lakeside has survived for more than a century as a Christian-oriented summer resort and a Catawba Island landmark.

Confluence of the Maumee and Auglaize Rivers, 1929 (Defiance County)

Local photographer Edward Bronson captured this view from the site of Fort Defiance, constructed by order of General "Mad" Anthony Wayne in 1794. The fort's square stockade, four blockhouses, 8-foot earth wall, and 8-foot-deep ditch led John Boyer, a lieutenant in Wayne's army, to claim that the fort could protect soldiers from "the English, the Indians, and all the devils in hell." After the Treaty of Greenville was signed in 1795, Fort Defiance was maintained as a trading post and fort within Indian territory and was used again by William Henry Harrison during the War of 1812. The city of Defiance was founded on the old fort's site.

The river confluence and viewing platform remain much as they were in 1929, although the surrounding area is much thicker with trees and other greenery.

PHOTOGRAPHER   *The shrubs in the foreground were in serious need of a trim by the park's grounds crew; in order to capture an unblocked view of the curved rail, I did some minor landscape maintenance, trimming off a couple of the larger shoots. The result is this lovely shot of an Ohio sunrise on a still river.*

Independence Dam, 1924 (Defiance County)

Just downstream from the confluence of the Maumee and Auglaize Rivers, Independence Dam State Park has links with both the Great Black Swamp and the canal system. The Maumee River valley was the last stronghold of the Black Swamp, with its monster hardwood trees and marshy forest floor. Also nearby was the junction of the Miami & Erie and the Wabash & Erie Canals. Independence Dam, shown here just after its construction in 1924, replaced a wooden canal dam.

The Maumee River valley still supports many descendants of the sycamore, locust, beech, and maple trees that blanketed the area when white settlers arrived. And although the Miami & Erie went out of business nearly a century ago, 7 unbroken miles of canal beds remain near Independence Dam, and the main entrance to Independence Dam State Park crosses the ruins of Lock 13.

Saint Augustine Church, Minster, 1948 (Auglaize County)

Visitors to Mercer and Auglaize Counties find more than cornstalks sprouting from the flat fields. Dozens of Gothic church steeples dot the horizon, attached to the many German Catholic churches in the region. St. Augustine Church in Minster was the "mother church" of the area. When built in 1848 to replace the original log church, a single steeple and the entrance were at the east end of the building. In 1874, the twin towers shown here were added to the west end and the original steeple was removed. Finally, in 1901, the entrance was moved to the west end of the church between the twin spires and the sanctuary was moved to the east end.

St. Augustine's has changed little since the first half of the twentieth century. The inset photo, taken approaching Minster, illustrates the prominence of the steeples in "The Land of the Cross-Tipped Churches." It is often possible to see several spires at once across the fields.

J. H. Manchester Barn, New Hampshire, circa 1909 (Auglaize County)

Agriculture is central to northwest Ohio, and good farmers don't stint on their outbuildings. The J. H. Manchester Barn was built in 1908 by Horace Duncan, whose name is proudly displayed above the door. The wooden barn is 102 feet in diameter and 80 feet tall—one of the largest round barns east of the Mississippi. The design allowed the farmer to store hay and feed in the center and easily distribute it to the animals housed around the perimeter.

Sporting a recent new roof and cheery red paint, the Manchester barn looks much the same today, though the surrounding outbuildings have changed and the nearby fields and fencerows are more open today than 80 years ago. This photo shows again the flat fields that are typical of northwest Ohio farm country. The barn is now used by the Manchester family for seed conditioning rather than to house farm animals.

Grand Lake St. Marys Canal Feeder Lock, 1913 (Auglaize County)

This feeder canal from Grand Lake St. Marys entered the Miami & Erie Canal just south of the city of St. Marys. Grand Lake St. Marys was the largest man-made lake in the world when it was completed as part of the Miami & Erie canal system in 1845 and remains the largest built without the use of machinery. This bulkhead lock controlled the flow of water between the lake and the 3-mile feeder. Ironically, this photo must have been taken a few weeks after the devastating flood of March 1913 that destroyed much of the Miami & Erie system.

Though the wooden lock gate is gone, the stone bulkhead looks much the same now as in 1913, and the small house at left still stands. The feeder stills fills sections of the old canal bed in St. Marys. The title of the "now" photo, "Gone Fishing," points to a pastime as popular today as it was then.

Miami & Erie Canal, St. Marys, 1919 (Auglaize County)

In 1919, this section of the canal through the city of St. Marys was flanked on the right by the Rapp Brothers livery stable, the St. Marys Telephone Company, and some private homes. The tall building at left is wedged between the canal and East Spring Street, which runs at about the same level as the bridge over the lock in the background. At the time of this photo, the canals were already nearly defunct.

Today the stretch of canal is St. Marys Memorial Park, with the *Belle of St. Marys* canal boat on permanent display. The lock in the background of the historic photo is now filled in, but a large section of the canal still runs through St. Marys, including a two-level section that cools the generators in the city's power plant, then splashes over a quaint stone spillway called "The Tumbles."

PHOTOGRAPHER *By the time I made it over to St. Marys Memorial Park to take this photo, it was turning dark and a severe thunderstorm was looming. Despite the threatening lightning, I decided to attempt a shot rather than have to stay overnight or make a two-hour return trip in the morning. I took my tripod somewhat reluctantly, but knew I would need it. When I arrived and saw the mule and canal boat so nicely lit in the evening light, I decided to quickly rephotograph the scene. Needless to say, I was very pleased with the result and did not return the next day.*

Washington Street Firehouse, New Bremen, circa 1890–1900 (Auglaize County)

Founded by German immigrants in 1832, New Bremen sat at the midpoint of the Miami & Erie Canal. The town boasted a number of gristmills, woolen mills, sawmills, packing plants, and grain warehouses near the canal. This elaborate firehouse and its neighboring commercial buildings reflected the town's prosperity in the late 1800s.

Today OH 66—Washington Street in New Bremen—follows the route of the old canal through Auglaize County. The old firehouse and its turreted neighbor are among the many beautifully restored canal-era buildings remaining in this picturesque canal town.

Courthouse Square, Sidney, circa 1886–1888 (Shelby County)

The Shelby County Courthouse was built between 1881 and 1883, one of many beautiful, ornate county courthouses in Ohio. A generous courthouse square with wide streets was the rule during this era, allowing space not only for traffic but often for weekly market stalls and community parades and events. The photo was taken when the courthouse was still very new and shows several of the commercial buildings surrounding the square.

This current photo is a good example of just how much the downtowns of many small Ohio cities remain as they were 100 years ago. The wide streets of the courthouse square have allowed modern multilane streets to be built without having to destroy the older buildings. Though the streets behind the courthouse are now mostly obscured by trees and signs, the corner building in the background is the same, as is the building at the far edge of the photo. Even the tiny corner of roof cornice still shows at the upper right.

Central Ohio

Agriculture and government, city and countryside, Virginia and New England: Central Ohio is the place where Ohio's diverse elements meet. Ohio's capital, Columbus, has been the state's central crossroads since its founding, when it served as the meeting point of the National Road and a major north-south Indian trail. Today the junction of I-70 and I-71 connects Columbus to Cleveland and Cincinnati and to points east and west.

Columbus is now Ohio's largest city, having surpassed Cleveland several years ago. Not surprisingly, government is a major employer in central Ohio, but Columbus is also a magnet for white-collar businesses such as insurance and technology firms. Historically, Columbus has also been a manufacturing center, serving as the base for the Jeffrey Manufacturing Company, once the world's leading maker of mining equipment, and for the state's largest buggy manufacturer, the Columbus Buggy Company. And, of course, as the home of The Ohio State University and several other universities and colleges, central Ohio is a major presence in higher education in the state and nationwide.

Outside of Columbus and its ring of fast-growing suburbs, however, central Ohio is still a place of small towns and farmland. To the east and northeast lie Granville and Mount Vernon, small towns built on

the New England model so common in northeast Ohio. To the southeast are Lancaster and Circleville, settled by Pennsylvanians and Southerners. Off to the northwest, Plain City—founded by German Mennonite farmers—and nearby Marysville are quickly being swallowed up by development, as is Delaware to the north. Farther out to the north and northwest, Marion and Bellefontaine remain small cities that are surrounded by farmland.

Central Ohio's landscape is also a mix, including remnants of the tall-grass prairies of western Ohio, sandstone gorges along the Licking River, and the edges of the unglaciated plateau that makes up southeast Ohio. The highest point in the state can also be found here, in the rolling hills of Logan County.

Perhaps it is fitting that the central area of the state and its capital should be such a perfect mix of diverse geography and cultural influences. Central Ohio is less its own unique area than the drawing together of the disparate parts of the Buckeye State into a unit—the bow that binds the package. It is indeed central to understanding the state's complex past and ever-changing present.

Ohio Theatre, Columbus, circa 1930

Ohio Statehouse, Columbus, circa 1865–1875 (Franklin County)

Begun in 1839 and finished in 1861, Ohio's Greek Revival statehouse, with its distinctive "wedding cake" cupola, dominated downtown Columbus when this photo was taken sometime before 1875. The relaxed pace of life in the capital is shown by the light horse traffic on State Street and the group of men leaning against the spiked iron fence surrounding the statehouse block.

Although its surrounding grounds still create an island of green in downtown Columbus, the statehouse is now dwarfed by the buildings surrounding it. The small building in the foreground houses stairs to the underground parking garage that now underlies the block. The statehouse itself underwent an extensive renovation in the 1990s. Dozens of offices that had been added to every available corner, including in former light wells and the "extra" space between the original floors, were removed and the interior returned to something like its original appearance.

North High Street, Columbus, circa 1895 (Franklin County)

In the late 1800s, Columbus was known as the "Arch City" for the lighted arches that bridged High and Main Streets. This photo was probably taken around 1895, when construction began on Columbus' third Union Depot, to the right of the fence. Note the large painted advertisement for C.R. Parish Co. on the building at the left.

Businesses and railroad terminals may come and go, but the C.R. Parish advertisement lives on more than a century after it was painted. The Union Depot was demolished in 1976 to make way for the Greater Columbus Convention Center, at right. Up the street is the city's attempt to revive the famous arches. The new arches were installed in 2002 at a cost of $1.5 million. They were originally designed with fiber-optic lights, but will be revamped due to technical glitches.

Gay Street Looking East from High Street, Columbus, circa 1900 (Franklin County)

This view of Gay Street is a bustle of pedestrians, streetcars, autos, and horses. The Keith Theatre is prominent on the north side of Gay Street, and the Gay Academy of Dance dominates the southeast corner of the intersection.

Today the Keith Theatre and the Academy of Dance are long gone, but other buildings in the old photo remain. The corner building at left looks much the same except for the inevitable modernized storefront; the building immediately behind it has changed little except for losing its awnings. The two buildings on either side of Pearl Alley (center right) have also survived. As for the bustle, the new photo is a bit deceptive: During weekdays, foot and auto traffic is much more reminiscent of the historical scene. This photo was taken on a weekend to avoid a clash between photographer and three lanes of westbound traffic.

Wyandotte Building, Columbus, circa 1895–1900 (Franklin County)

In 1894, the Wyandotte Building was Columbus' first modern, steel-framed skyscraper. Architect Daniel Burnham also designed the Flatiron Building in New York City and dozens of other famous buildings of his age. The Wyandotte's bay windows allowed maximum light to enter from crowded city streets—ironically unnecessary in this early photo when the Wyandotte was the tallest building in the city and required awnings to control the light from the west.

The Wyandotte has survived its neighbors, but barely registers on the skyline of modern Columbus. Surrounded by enormous structures like the Huntington Center (at right), the Wyandotte's bay windows are possibly more useful today than in the past. In this afternoon shot, the western light is now blocked by a taller neighbor in lieu of awnings.

Ohio State Penitentiary, Columbus, circa 1900–1910 (Franklin County)

Not all of Columbus' historic buildings have survived into the twenty-first century. Opened in 1834, the Ohio Penitentiary eventually spread over 26 acres at Spring Street and Neil Avenue (then Dennison Avenue). During its long existence, the Pen (as it was known) sheltered the famous and the infamous, including Confederate general John Hunt Morgan, who embarrassed the prison administration by escaping under their noses with several of his men; short-story writer O. Henry; and Dr. Sam Sheppard, who was later cleared in the murder of his wife, Marilyn. In 1930, it was also the site of the worst prison fire in U.S. history, when 322 inmates were killed in two cell blocks along the west side of the complex.

The aging penitentiary was closed in 1984 and demolished by the City of Columbus in 1998, despite efforts by local architects and preservationists to save at least a part of the facade for reuse in future redevelopment. Today what remains of the fine stonework of the facade lies scattered in a local stone yard, and offices, parking garages, and condominiums are rising where cell blocks and Old Sparky once stood.

Franklin Park Conservatory, Columbus, circa 1894–1897 (Franklin County)

From 1851 to 1884, the Franklin Park area was the Ohio State Fairgrounds. In 1886, it became a public park. Eight years later, Columbus and Franklin County erected this fine iron-and-glass conservatory building and filled it with palms and other plants foreign to Midwestern Columbus. The citizens of Victorian-age Columbus flocked to see the exotic flora. This photo was taken within a few years of the conservatory's completion.

Though the landscaping has changed considerably, the exterior of Franklin Park Conservatory remains much the same after more than a century. The only significant difference is the main entryway, which was removed in the 1950s and replaced with a purely functional aluminum and glass structure. That structure was removed in its turn and replaced with a facsimile of the original structure that is slightly different in scale and proportion.

Old Ohio Deaf School, Columbus, 1974 (Franklin County)

This 1974 view of the old Ohio Deaf School facility graphically illustrates the changes in Columbus in only 30 years. The main building of the old Deaf School, at right, burned to the ground in the early 1980s. At center in the background is the LeVeque Tower, the most distinctive feature of Columbus' skyline since its completion in 1927.

Today the old Deaf School parking lot is the Topiary Garden, inhabited by topiary figures that recreate the Georges Seurat painting *A Sunday Afternoon on the Island of La Grande Jatte* (center left). The remaining Deaf School building, now offices, stands next to the expanded Columbus Metropolitan Library. The LeVeque Tower is still visible slightly to the right of center, but from this direction appears shrunken next to the likes of the Vern Riffe Center, the Huntington Center, the James A. Rhodes State Office Tower, and the dozens of other office buildings that have sprung up downtown. The inset photo shows the pond and several topiary figures in the Topiary Garden.

PHOTOGRAPHER   *I took the current view from the roof of the Washington Place Apartments. Unfortunately, two large trees now block the view from the spot where the earlier photograph was taken, so I had to change my position on the rooftop, which prevented an exact match. One can still appreciate the remarkable changes to Columbus in such a short period of time.*

Columbus Riverfront, circa 1940s (Franklin County)

Columbus' Scioto riverfront was once crowded to the waterline with ramshackle industrial buildings, which were wiped away in the great flood of 1913. The city seized the chance to build floodwalls and a planned civic center complex. The low, columned building at left is part of the city office complex, which included City Hall and the central police station. The rectangular building beyond the Broad Street Bridge is the Ohio State Office Building, an Art Deco masterpiece. The tower is the American Insurance Union Citadel, the tallest building in the state when it was finished in 1927 and probably Columbus' most widely recognized building after the Ohio Statehouse.

This view across the Scioto River is still one of Columbus' most beautiful. The civic center is still in use, though a new central police headquarters stands at left (with the green roof). The AIU Citadel is now the LeVeque Tower and joined by three challengers for skyline prominence: to its left is the James A. Rhodes State Office Tower; just to its right is the Huntington Center, and to the right of that is the Vern Riffe Center, another state office building. The former state office building has been renovated and is now occupied by the Ohio Supreme Court.

University Hall, The Ohio State University, 1937 (Franklin County)

The Ohio Agricultural and Mechanical College opened its doors in 1873, boasting seven faculty members and 25 students, including one female. From that inauspicious beginning grew The Ohio State University, which in 2002 had nearly 50,000 students enrolled at the Columbus campus alone and offers more than 10,000 courses through 18 colleges and schools.

OSU's first building, University Hall, was completed in 1874 and served as dormitory, faculty residence, and chapel, as well as class and administrative space. Student quarters were spartan, but so lively that they were quickly nicknamed "Purgatory" and the residents "imps." A favorite student prank was to creep upstairs to the faculty quarters, or "Saints' Roost," in the dead of night and pummel with pillows any faculty member gullible enough to answer a knock on his door. University Hall still holds its prominent place on OSU's Oval, but the close observer will notice a difference that caused Randall some interesting problems aligning this new shot with the old. The most obvious change is that parking is no longer allowed in front of the building, but the automobiles help mask the real kicker: University Hall is a half story shorter these days.

PHOTOGRAPHER *At the time I rephotographed University Hall, it concealed a fiendish little secret. I immediately noticed that the parking lot in the foreground was gone, but I also made a more per-plexing observation: In the old photo, there was a*

large staircase leading to an elevated entryway. As I looked through my viewfinder, I realized the front door I saw in front of me was at ground level. How could that be? I wondered. Had the ground level been raised? Was the building sinking like the Tower of Pisa or the Palace of Fine Arts in Mexico City? Looking at the towers and architectural details, it occurred to me that perhaps this was not the building in the old photograph. But not until that evening, when I confirmed that the original University Hall had been demolished and replaced by a close facsimile in 1974, was I willing to throw out my more interesting theories.

Orton Hall, The Ohio State University, 1895 (Franklin County)

Orton Hall's bell tower is, for many, the image of the Ohio State campus. This photo was taken about two years after the building was completed in 1893. Since it was to house the Geology department, the building's construction reflected its use. The exterior is entirely native Ohio stone, graduated by its geological age from oldest (the foundation) to newest (the upper walls). The decorative gargoyles above the upper ring of tower windows each represent an extinct Ohio animal.

Orton Hall's exterior has changed little during its century of use: The row of skylights at the roof peak is gone and the tower is enclosed against the weather and to protect its chimes. The buggy path that once passed by the door is now a parking area. Still the home of OSU's geological museum and its enormous skeleton of a three-toed sloth, Orton Hall is one of four campus buildings listed on the National Register of Historic Places.

Ohio Stadium, The Ohio State University, circa 1930s (Franklin County)

 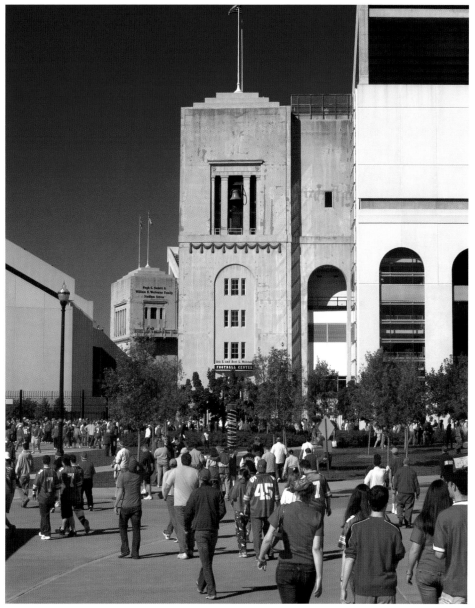

Ohio Stadium was completed in 1922 and is probably OSU's best-known structure, with an unusual open-ended design that earned it the nickname "The Horseshoe." When this photo was taken, the area around the stadium was still gardens and open space, but the Buckeyes' football games were already drawing huge crowds, albeit dressed a bit formally to modern eyes.

Extensive renovations in the 1990s lowered the football field and encased most of the original stadium in a new structure that added hundreds of seats and new luxury boxes. The towers at the open end of the 'Shoe are among the few parts of the original stadium still visible from the outside and comprise one of the few views that can be reshot today, due to encroaching buildings and construction around the stadium. One thing, at least, has not changed: Football Saturdays still draw the crowds.

Harding Memorial, Marion, 1931 (Marion County)

Ohio has been home to eight U.S. presidents: William Henry Harrison, Ulysses S. Grant, Rutherford B. Hayes, James A. Garfield, Benjamin Harrison, William McKinley, William Howard Taft, and Warren G. Harding. Of the eight, Warren Harding was arguably the least distinguished, presiding over a scandal-ridden administration before dying in office in 1923. Despite his lackluster presidency, public donations funded this magnificent Georgia marble memorial on a 10-acre site in Marion, where Harding had been a newspaper publisher. The remains of Harding and his wife Florence were interred in the finished memorial in 1927, and formal dedication ceremonies (shown here) were held in 1931.

One of the most beautiful presidential memorials to be found outside of Washington, D.C., the Harding Memorial is more than 50 feet tall and 103 feet in diameter. Its 46 Doric columns and open design resemble a Greek temple. The site is now cared for by the Ohio Historical Society, which also administers the restored Harding home in Marion.

Piatt Castle Mac-O-Chee, circa 1910 (Logan County)

Piatt Castle Mac-O-Chee, finished in 1881, was the home of Civil War colonel, journalist, and social critic Donn Piatt and his wife, Ella Kirby Piatt. Donn's brother, General Abram Piatt, had already built his own limestone "castle" nearby, named Mac-A-Cheek. While Mac-A-Cheek passed to Abram's descendants, Mac-O-Chee was sold and used at various times as a health spa, a storage barn for farm equipment, and a museum.

Today Mac-O-Chee is again owned by the Piatts. Without its thick covering of ivy, the castle's steep, stepped, Flemish-style gables and tower are visible, as well as the center section that joins the original 1866 cottage to the left. The rolling hills around the two castles have changed little since Donn Piatt's time; cornfields still surround the two homes and the wooded hill of the nearby family cemetery. Both Mac-O-Chee and Mac-A-Cheek are being restored by the Piatt family and are open for tours, programs, and rentals.

Main Street, Lancaster (Fairfield County)

This series of photos along Main Street in Lancaster shows an interesting progression of renovations over the years. Lancaster is probably best known as the home of Judge Charles Sherman and the birthplace of his two famous sons, Senator John Sherman and General William Tecumseh Sherman. In the mid-1800s, Lancaster was a thriving canal and railroad town. The Hotel Mithoff, at right in the photos, began its life in 1866 as a brick Federalist-style structure, but even in 1867, when the older photo was taken, it sported an arched Italianate storefront. By 1870, the roof had been raised and flattened and Italianate cornice supports added. Farther down the street is the tower of the old Lancaster City Hall.

Today the Hotel Mithoff building looks much as it did in 1879 from the second story up, but the once-stylish Italianate facade has been replaced by modern plate-glass windows. The tower of the "new" City Hall, built in 1872, shows near the left side of the photo. Though Lancaster's Main Street shares the all-too-common vacant buildings of a small downtown bypassed by a major highway, the current attractive streetscape is surely more inviting than this description of Main Street in 1874, found in the *Lancaster Gazette*: "The gutters are choked up with watermelon rinds, waste paper and rubbish....The inevitable picture presented on Main Street, on these sweltering afternoons, has been a battalion of geese marching down the sidewalk with exasperating impunity, a cow or so, a half dozen dogs before every basement entrance, and every corner festooned with a brigade of swine."

1870

Circleville Pumpkin Show, Circleville, 1906 (Pickaway County)

The city of Circleville was originally laid out in 1810 entirely within a huge circular earthwork, probably a remnant of the prehistoric Hopewell people. After about 30 years, citizen complaints about the peculiar radial layout of the streets led to "squaring" the town. Circleville is now best known for its annual Pumpkin Show, founded in 1903 when Mayor George Haswell invited local farmers to display their wares in front of the waterworks office. The event, seen here in 1906, quickly became a showcase for local farmers and other businesses as well—hence the large display of locally made Eagle Mops at right.

Over the last decades, the Pumpkin Show has added carnival rides and parades, but the biggest draw remains the pumpkins. In recent years, the show has brought around 400,000 visitors annually to downtown Circleville, where many of the old buildings that witnessed the first show more than a century ago still stand. At center right, the Pythian Castle and the attached building to its right have survived with only one turret missing and the seemingly inevitable renovated storefronts; the second building to the left of the Castle also remains.

PHOTOGRAPHER *I've been photographing the Circleville Pumpkin Show for many years, and I thought it would make an interesting "then and now" if we could find an early photograph taken down Court Street. We found the 1906 picture, and I rephotographed the scene at a recent festival from ground level, as in the old photo. However, after seeing the results, I decided to use this present-day view instead. It was taken a year earlier from an elevated position with a better view of the crowds and pumpkins. The largest champion pumpkin when I first started photographing the festival weighed about 500 lbs. If you look closely you can see that the record-breaking pumpkin in this photo weighed more than 1,300 pounds. In 2005, the champion tipped the scales at over 1,400 pounds!*

Buxton Inn, Granville, circa 1860s (Licking County)

Granville is a charming New England–style town east of Columbus, filled with beautifully kept historic buildings and residences. The Buxton Inn, one of the best known, was a stagecoach stop when it opened in 1812. The old inn has at various times housed classrooms, church services, and the local courts. Today it is Ohio's oldest continuously operated inn still in its original building. The Buxton's rooms have sheltered the likes of William McKinley, Henry Ward Beecher, and Harriet Beecher Stowe, as well as thousands of guests less famous.

Current innkeepers Orville and Audrey Orr bought the Buxton Inn in 1972 and spent two years on updates and renovation. The distinctive coral paint on the exterior is historically accurate, and the building is filled with period antiques. Besides its guests and restaurant patrons, the Buxton is widely reputed to harbor several inhabitants from its past, including at least two former innkeepers and a friendly spirit cat, the inspiration for the inn's modern-day sign.

PHOTOGRAPHER *Pictured are Audrey and Orville Orr, daughter Amy, and grandchildren Simon and Oliver along with several current staff members. The only way I could rephotograph the inn from a similar view was to move in closer, changing the perspective but also forcing me to include the pole.*

Broadway, Granville, circa 1955 (Licking County)

The second half of the twentieth century brought huge changes to cities and towns across Ohio, but many small cities like Granville have retained their busy, charming downtowns with little change. This photo from around 1955 shows the north side of Broadway with its row of narrow nineteenth-century Italianate commercial buildings sporting cloth awnings to protect storefronts from the sun.

Fifty years later, only the paint and awnings on the fronts of the buildings have changed; even the large tree at the left remains. Granville has worked hard to maintain its historic character in the face of encroaching development from Columbus and Newark and has so far mostly resisted the strip mall developments that have emptied so many Main Streets across the state.

ISBN-10: 1-56579-546-6 • ISBN-13: 978-1-56579-546-4

CONTEMPORARY PHOTOGRAPHY: Randall Lee Schieber, ©2006. All rights reserved.
TEXT: Robin Smith and Randall Lee Schieber, ©2006. All rights reserved.
EDITOR: Jennifer Jahner
DESIGN: Rebecca Finkel, F + P Graphic Design, Inc.
PRODUCTION MANAGER: Craig Keyzer

PUBLISHED BY:
Westcliffe Publishers, Inc., P.O. Box 1261, Englewood, CO 80150
westcliffepublishers.com

Printed in China through World Print, Ltd.

For more information about other fine books and calendars from Westcliffe Publishers, please contact your local bookstore, call us at 1-800-523-3692, or visit us on the Web at **westcliffepublishers.com**.

About the Photographer and Author

RANDALL LEE SCHIEBER is a commercial photographer based in Columbus, Ohio. He specializes in architectural, landscape, editorial, and travel photography. His work has appeared in numerous national and local publications, including *Midwest Living, Ohio Magazine, The New York Times,* and *Audubon.* He has published several calendars on Ohio and is featured every year exclusively in the Ohio Scenic Calendar. He is currently working on a book about Columbus, which will add to several published books on Ohio that showcase his work.

Schieber was born in Findlay, Ohio. His early childhood was spent in Mexico City, where he learned to speak Spanish and developed an interest in travel. He has traveled widely throughout the United States and Mexico. He studied photography and art, first in Tucson, Arizona, and later at The Ohio State University in Columbus. He earned a B.A. from Kent State University.

ROBIN SMITH is a writer and graphic artist. She spent 18 years in the design field, including a seven-year stint as a design and production artist for *Ohio Magazine,* where her primary focus was Ohio travel and tourism publications. Smith is now a partner in Emuses Press, a small press and design firm in Columbus, Ohio. She is the author of *Columbus Ghosts: Historical Haunts of Ohio's Capital* and *Columbus Ghosts II: More Central Ohio Haunts,* which combine local ghost lore with Columbus history, and is currently working on a collection of Ohio disaster stories.

Smith was born in Dayton, Ohio, and is a lifelong resident of the state. She earned a B.A. in art at Wright State University in Fairborn, Ohio, where she studied drawing and photography. In addition to Ohio history and ghosts, her interests include gardening, genealogy, and traveling with her husband and daughter.

LIBRARY OF CONGRESS CATALOGING-IN-PUBLICATION DATA
Schieber, Randall Lee
  Ohio then & now : contemporary rephotography / by Randall Lee Schieber ; text by Robin Smith and Randall Lee Schieber.
    p. cm.
    ISBN-13: 978-1-56579-546-4
    ISBN-10: 1-56579-546-6
    1. Ohio—Pictorial works. 2. Ohio—History--Pictorial works. 3. Ohio—History, Local—Pictorial works. 4. Repeat photography—Ohio. I. Smith, Robin. II. Title. III. Title: Ohio then and now.
  F492.S346 2006
  977.1—dc22
                          2006012985

Photography Credits

OHIO: CONTRASTS AND CROSSROADS
Elephants in Dayton Special Collections and Archives, Wright State University Libraries
Train Depot, Zanesville Pioneer and Historical Society of Muskingum County

SOUTHEAST
Stockport Mill Pickenpaugh Studio, Caldwell, Ohio
Wreck of the *Shenandoah* near Ava Pickenpaugh Studio, Caldwell, Ohio
Marietta from Harmar Hill From *Views of Washington County,* courtesy Art Smith
Ohio River Levee Slack Research Collections, Dawes Memorial Library, Marietta College
Williamstown Bridge Slack Research Collections, Dawes Memorial Library, Marietta College
Confluence of the Ohio and Muskingum Rivers From *Views of Washington County,* courtesy Art Smith
Lock 3, Lowell Pickenpaugh Studio, Caldwell, Ohio
McConnelsville Opera House Pickenpaugh Studio, Caldwell, Ohio
Muskingum County Courthouse Pioneer and Historical Society of Muskingum County
Zanesville 1: Pioneer and Historical Society of Muskingum County; 2: Library of Congress, Prints and Photographs Division
Y-bridge, Zanesville 1 and 2: Ohio Historical Society
S-bridge, New Concord Ohio Historical Society
National Road Pickenpaugh Studio, Caldwell, Ohio
Conkle's Hollow State Nature Preserve Ohio Historical Society
Trail to Lower Falls, Old Man's Cave Ohio Historical Society
Rock House Ohio Historical Society
Cedar Falls Ohio Historical Society
Ohio University Alumni Gate Athens County Historical Society
Court Street, Athens Anastas Collection, Athens County Historical Society
Athens Lunatic Asylum Robert E. and Jean R. Mahn Center for Archives and Special Collections, Ohio University Libraries
Canaan Coal Company Store Athens County Historical Society
Ross County Courthouse Ross County Historical Society
Adena 1 and 2: Ohio Historical Society
Ohio River and Floodwall Carl Ackerman Collection, Southern Ohio Museum
Ohio River and General U. S. Grant Bridge Carl Ackerman Collection, Southern Ohio Museum
Columbia Theatre Carl Ackerman Collection, Southern Ohio Museum
Sciotoville Railroad Bridge Ohio Historical Society
Park Central Hotel David Tawney Studio, Gallipolis, Ohio
Gallipolis from Fortification Hill David Tawney Studio/Larry Betz, Gallipolis, Ohio
2nd Avenue, Gallipolis David Tawney Studio, Gallipolis, Ohio

NORTHEAST
Main Street, Baltic Brooks Harris Collection
Public Square Library of Congress, Prints and Photographs Division
Euclid Avenue at Playhouse Square Western Reserve Historical Society
East 9th Street Pier Western Reserve Historical Society
Rocky River Marina Western Reserve Historical Society
Ashtabula Harbor Ashtabula Marine Museum
Harpersfield Bridge Harpersfield Heritage Society
Howard Street Hill University of Akron Archival Services

Downtown Akron with Quaker Oats Enlarging Arts, Inc.
English Garden, Stan Hywet Hall Stan Hywet Hall and Garden Archives
Goodyear Airdock The Bronson Collection, Defiance Public Library
Central Square Mahoning Valley Historical Society
Steubenville from Moodey's Hill Public Library of Steubenville and Jefferson County/Schiappa Branch
Court and Market Streets Public Library of Steubenville and Jefferson County/Schiappa Branch
North Street Fire Station Public Library of Steubenville and Jefferson County/Schiappa Branch
East Liverpool and Ohio River Ohio Historical Society Museum of Ceramics/East Liverpool Historical Society
Thompson Block Ohio Historical Society Museum of Ceramics/East Liverpool Historical Society
5th Street, East Liverpool 1 and 2: Ohio Historical Society Museum of Ceramics/East Liverpool Historical Society
Brandywine Falls Peninsula Library and Historical Society
Lanterman's Mill Mahoning Valley Historical Society
Alexander/Wilson Feed Mill University of Akron Archival Services
Mustill Store University of Akron Archival Services
Magnolia Flouring Mill University of Akron Archival Services
Main Street, Millersburg Brooks Harris Collection
Zoar Hotel Ohio Historical Society
Zoar School Ohio Historical Society
Big House, Malabar Farm Ohio Department of Natural Resources
Memorial Forest Shrine Ohio Department of Natural Resources, Division of Forestry

SOUTHWEST
Miami & Erie Canal Looking North from 5th Street Dayton Metro Library
Montgomery County Courthouse Dayton Metro Library
Cincinnati from the John A. Roebling Suspension Bridge Library of Congress, Prints and Photographs Division
Cincinnati Union Terminal 1 and 2: Cincinnati Museum Center/Cincinnati Historical Society Library
Miami & Erie Canal/Central Parkway Cincinnati Museum Center/Cincinnati Historical Society Library
A Sunday Afternoon in Cincinnati's Eden Park Cincinnati Museum Center/Cincinnati Historical Society Library
Ohio River From Eden Park Ohio Historical Society
Miami & Erie Canal Looking North from Green Street Special Collections and Archives, Wright State University Libraries
Memorial Hall Montgomery County Historical Society
Wright Brothers Flight at Huffman Prairie Special Collections and Archives, Wright State University Libraries
Englewood Dam Special Collections and Archives, Wright State University Libraries
Crowell-Collier Clark County Historical Society
Bushnell House Clark County Public Library
Rankin House Ohio Historical Society
Commercial Square Courtesy Marvin Case, Old Timers Building
Bailey House Courtesy Marvin Case, Old Timers Building
Mariemont Cincinnati Museum Center/Cincinnati Historical Society Library
Spring Grove Lake and Chapel 1 and 2: Paul Briol Collection, Spring Grove Cemetery and Arboretum
Seven Caves Ohio Historical Society
Serpent Mound Bert Highlands Collection, Mechanicsburg Public Library
Cascades, Glen Helen Montgomery County Historical Society
The Golden Lamb Warren County Historical Society
Public Square, Troy Ohio Historical Society

NORTHWEST
4-H Club Excursion Sandusky Library Follett House Museum Archives
Interurban Bridge and Roche de Boeuf Bowling Green State University Center for Archival Collections
Toledo Riverfront Toledo–Lucas County Library Legacy Foundation
Maumee River and Cherry Street Bridge Toledo–Lucas County Library Legacy Foundation
Superior Street, Toledo Toledo–Lucas County Library Legacy Foundation
Marathon Oil Building Hancock Historical Museum
Main Street Looking North from Crawford Street Hancock Historical Museum; inset: Hancock Historical Museum
Main Street and First Lutheran Church From *Findlay Illustrated 1889,* courtesy Linda Paul
Kimmel and Boger Residences From *Findlay Illustrated 1889,* courtesy Linda Paul
Put-in-Bay Harbor and Mystic Isle Rutherford B. Hayes Presidential Center Library
Put-in-Bay Harbor and Perry's Victory and International Peace Memorial postcard by E. B. Ackley
Miller Boat Dock Rutherford B. Hayes Presidential Center Library
Marblehead Lighthouse U.S. Coast Guard
Interurban Bridge and Roche de Boeuf Bowling Green State University Center for Archival Collections
Lakeside Dock and Beach House The Lakeside Heritage Society
Confluence of the Maumee and Auglaize Rivers Bronson Collection/Defiance Public Library
Independence Dam Bronson Collection/Defiance Public Library
Saint Augustine Church Maria Stein Heritage Museum
J. H. Manchester Round Barn Manchester Family Archives
Grand Lake St. Marys Canal Feeder Lock George Neargarder Collection
Miami & Erie Canal, St. Marys George Neargarder Collection
Washington Street Firehouse New Bremen Historic Association
Courthouse Square Ohio Historical Society

CENTRAL
Ohio Theatre from *The Ohio Theatre, 1928–1978,* © 1978, Columbus Association for the Performing Arts
Ohio Statehouse Ohio Historical Society
North High Street Ohio Historical Society
Gay Street Looking East from High Street Ohio Historical Society
Wyandotte Building Ohio Historical Society
Ohio State Penitentiary Columbus Metropolitan Library Circulating Visuals Collection
Franklin Park Conservatory Columbus Metropolitan Library Circulating Visuals Collection
Old Ohio Deaf School Friends of the Topiary Park
Columbus Riverfront Ohio Historical Society
University Hall Ohio State University Archives
Orton Hall Ohio State University Archives
Ohio Stadium Ohio State University Archives
Harding Memorial Ohio Historical Society
Piatt Castle Mac-O-Chee Piatt Family Archives
Main Street, Lancaster 1 and 2: Ohio Historical Society
Circleville Pumpkin Show Pickaway County Historical and Genealogical Society
Buxton Inn Granville Historical Society
Broadway, Granville Granville Historical Society